The STORM GOURMET

The STORM GOURMET

A Guide to Creating Extraordinary Meals
WITHOUT ELECTRICITY

DAPHNE NIKOLOPOULOS

Pineapple Press, Inc.
SARASOTA, FLORIDA

Inquiries should be addressed to:

Pineapple Press, Inc.
P.O. Box 3889
Sarasota, Florida 34230

www.pineapplepress.com

Library of Congress Cataloging-in-Publication Data

Nikolopoulos, Daphne
  The storm gourmet : a guide to creating extraordinary meals without electricity / Daphne Nikolopoulos.-- 1st ed.
      p. cm.
  Includes bibliographical references and index.
  ISBN-13: 978-1-56164-334-9 (pbk. : alk. paper)
  ISBN-10: 1-56164-334-3 (pbk. : alk. paper)
  1. Cookery (Canned foods) 2. Menus. 3. Emergency management. I. Title: Meals without electricity. II. Title.
  TX821.N55 2005
  641.6'12--dc22

                                    2005015228

First Edition
10 9 8 7 6 5 4 3 2 1

Design by ospreyDESIGN, www.ospreydesign.com
Photography by Sigvision
Printed in Canada

Pineapple Press books are available at special quantity discounts to use as premiums or promotions or for use in training programs. For more information, write to Director of Special Sales, Pineapple Press, P.O. Box 3889, Sarasota, FL 34230. Or call 800-746-2375. Or contact your local bookseller.

For Toula,
the kitchen goddess

"If necessity is the mother of invention,
then resourcefulness is the father."
—*Beulah Louise Henry, U.S. inventor*

Acknowledgments

*T*hough it isn't always easy to see the positive side of foul weather, I gratefully and humbly acknowledge Mother Nature for bringing out the best in human nature. In 2004, when four hurricanes slammed into Florida and the Caribbean islands with impunity, individuals and communities came together in the face of peril. Neighbors helped neighbors batten down and, later, rebuild. People generously shared their resources with strangers. Utility staff worked long after dark for weeks to restore power. In short, we learned we are survivors and can be surprisingly resourceful when the chips are down.

This book is an example of that resourcefulness. Being without electricity for two weeks made me miss hot showers and freshly brewed coffee, but it also made me realize I'm not dependent on them. I began to contemplate how to do things differently and discovered that everything, down to how we eat, is part of life's ever-changing scenery. I am deeply grateful for that lesson.

I would like to thank June and David Cussen, and everyone at Pineapple Press, for believing in this book; Sig Bokalders for his talent and friendship; Carey O'Donnell for her energy, enthusiasm, and amazing ideas; Herb Perez–Vidal for his culinary expertise and constructive criticism; Paige Bowers for her help with research and her unconditional encouragement; and Scott Sanford for urging me to write in the first place. Very special thanks to all my friends and family who tasted and critiqued every single recipe; to the forecasters at Colorado State University for generously sharing information; to

Pasta USA for providing samples and listening to my crazy ideas; to Mary Lambert, PhD, for her guidance with herbs; to the USDA staff for their input on emergency food management; and to everyone who consented to interviews, often at short notice, and provided valuable input. Most of all, I thank my husband, Peter Lioubin, for being my rock through stormy weather, and for his ideas, vision, and loving support through the development of this book.

Table of Contents

Introduction

If you live in an area that is prone to storms or other natural calamities, chances are you can relate to the reasons this book was created. Hurricanes, blizzards, tsunamis and the rest of nature's tantrums strike without remorse, and often without warning, leaving in their wake unpleasant consequences from minor inconvenience to all-out disaster.

During a major weather event, the critical decisions of securing life and property are complicated by disruptions in critical resources like electricity. Storms aren't the only culprits in electrical sabotage; power loss can occur due to an alarmingly long list of reasons: earthquakes, tornados, terrorist attacks, taxed resources due to growing populations, and even aging grids. When power is down, life as we know it comes to an abrupt halt.

In life, rainy days are aplenty; but as the popular slogan goes, "You gotta eat." Granted, when stress is running high and survival mode kicks in, the last thing anyone wants to do is make a fuss in the kitchen. There are far more pressing things to do. But nutrition and nourishment are particularly important during stressful times. And no one can argue that an enjoyable meal helps alleviate stress.

The problem is, it's hard to eat like a gourmand when you are limited to the supermarket's instant-food aisle. Let's face it: Canned stew, powdered milk, and tuna aren't exactly the makings of a Dionysian feast.

Unless, of course, you know what to do with them.

The Storm Gourmet is the answer to the perennial question, "What to have for dinner?" when resources are extremely limited. Most of us don't know what to do without Direct TV, let alone how to get by without refrigeration, oven, coffeemaker, food processor or electrical gadgets of any kind. And when we are faced with a cupboard full of nonperishables, our first instinct is to open up a can and stoically consume the contents like contestants on Fear Factor. Is it possible to create well-balanced, tasty meals under such circumstances? Of course it is! After all, our forebears did it—and they didn't have half the raw materials we have today.

This book is not so much a cookbook as a guide to disaster preparedness from a culinary perspective. In the event of a storm— or any emergency—food often is relegated to the proverbial back burner, partly because there is precious little time to cook, but mostly because of inadequate planning. Most people realize far too late that all they've got to work with are a few cans of baked beans, some beef jerky, and a bunch of candy bars. This book tells you how to stock your pantry well in advance of the onslaught of storm season, how to substitute your kitchen tools with nonelectrical equivalents, and how to combine shelf-stable foods and fresh ingredients from your garden with delicious results. It even gives you menu suggestions to help you create everything from a romantic picnic to a Florida-style buffet for the entire family.

The recipes contained herein have been tested in our kitchens, and subsequently tasted—and enthusiastically approved—by a gamut of individuals, from food critics to kids. Some have an ethnic flair; others put a new spin on familiar favorites. All are simple and easy to prepare, as they require absolutely no temperature cooking—so you can move on to more important things. If a heat source, such as a grill, is available, many of these recipes can easily be adapted. For example, you may use fresh grilled chicken instead of the packaged variety, or you may substitute traditional pasta for the instant pasta suggested here.

This method of cooking is applicable not only to natural and man-made disasters, but also to any situation where electricity is not available—camping, sailing, you name it. What's more, it's useful beyond emergency situations. How many times have you had someone drop by, or have come home late from work, when there is nothing in the fridge and no time to run to the store? By following the provisioning guide and recipes in *The Storm Gourmet*, you can always whip up an impressive snack or meal—in practically no time.

These meals are so effortless, wholesome, and delicious that they are bound to become family favorites even in fair-weather days. And when storm season comes 'round, batten down, and check emergency reports to see whether you are in an evacuation area. If you are safe to ride out the storm at home, stock up. No matter where the wind blows, you will be prepared—to eat well. We hope you will enjoy the compilation of recipes, advice, and anecdotes in the pages that follow.

Getting Prepared

A Florida old-timer once said that hurricanes are nature's way of making us slow down and appreciate the fact that we are not, as we sometimes deceive ourselves into believing, at the top of the food chain. Mother Nature is boss, he liked to say, and she will not hesitate to put us in our place.

Like taxes, natural disasters are one of life's certainties. People who live on the coastal regions of the Atlantic Ocean and the Gulf of Mexico have learned to take hurricanes very seriously. Each winter, residents of the northeastern United States and parts of the Midwest brace themselves for the onslaught of blizzards and snowstorms. In earthquake-battered California, people live with the prospect of The Big One wreaking havoc.

Natural disasters, from major hurricanes to tsunamis to volcanic eruptions, make headlines on an all-too-regular basis. These and other crises, such as terrorist attacks, have the potential to displace people, ravage homes, destroy infrastructures, and leave in their wake the chaos that typically results from loss of basic necessities. One of those basics, which most of us take for granted, is electricity. As millions of Americans who have lived through emergency situations can attest, the lack of power is not merely an annoyance we can laugh off or circumvent. Electricity is so enmeshed in our daily lives that without it, we have to retrain ourselves to exist using our own wits and resourcefulness.

For most people, these words probably will not register—until they actually experience nature's wrath firsthand. Let us describe a typical scenario.

The weatherman has been talking about a big storm looming off the coast for several days. Suddenly, the television monitor shows the cone of probability—or, plainly put, the storm's projected path—sweeping right over your backyard in forty-eight hours. What's worse, the storm

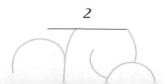

has been upgraded to a Category Three hurricane—and it's gaining strength as it churns through tropical waters.

What do you do now? Why, panic, of course. You kick yourself because you never bought those storm shutters, then drive to your local home-improvement store to find this sign in the plywood department: "Sold Out." Curiously, you see the same sign every-where—the gas station, the battery racks at the hardware store, the generator aisle at the tool rental center, and on it goes. "OK," you think to yourself, "I can always haul the family out of town." But one look at the interstate (or is that a parking lot?), combined with the earlier visual of the "Sold Out" sign at the gas station, convinces you otherwise. You call the airlines. Flight to Las Vegas? Full. Alaska? Canceled. Timbuktu? Plenty of seats, at three thousand dollars each.

Realizing there's no escape, you begin to think about food and water. You run to the store, only to get another reality check. The supermarket stampede brings to mind images of the Klondike during Gold Rush: The shelves have been mined, the goods have been picked over, and the lines are as long as the Yukon. From the dark recesses of your mind surfaces your old Scout motto—Be prepared!—and it dawns on you that maybe you should have antic-ipated this moment and planned ahead.

Though it is not within our power to control the violent moods of nature, we do have the ability to prepare for a disaster situation and its potentially chaotic aftermath. The natural reaction of human beings threatened with impending doom is to panic. That's why proper preparation is so important. Not only do you save yourself the stress, you also avoid the frantic masses going *mano a mano* for the last package of tuna in the canned goods aisle.

While this book does not purport to be the definitive disaster preparedness guide, it will help you prepare your kitchen for the eventuality of electricity loss so that you and your family can enjoy wholesome—and, yes, delicious—meals during and after a time of crisis. By having a plan and following these carefully thought-out recipes, you can circumvent the usual panic-purchases of, say, canned ravioli or Spam, which usually lead to disastrous meals and questionable nutrition. This chapter explains what and how much to buy, when to buy it and how to store it, as well as the importance of enhancing flavor with spices, fresh herbs and, if available, fruit from the backyard tree.

The idea is to prepare for the worst, and hope for the best. Even if a direct hit never comes—and let's hope it doesn't—your biggest dilemma will be what to do with all the emergency supplies in your pantry. That's where *The Storm Gourmet* comes in. Emergency supplies are the star ingredients in these recipes—so, even after electricity service resumes, nothing will go to waste. The recipes may be designed for disaster conditions, but are so simple to execute and so yummy that they offer quick meal solutions year-round.

*S*tore food in a cool, dry place. Because storms carry the risk of flooding, keep food supplies on shelves or cabinets well above floor level and away from unprotected windows, which may break and admit water. Remember, the garage will probably be the first to flood. If you choose to keep your food stock in the garage, ensure it is off the floor and away from the door. If food, including canned goods, or water comes in contact with floodwater, it must be discarded.

The Well-Stocked Storm Pantry
Meal Plans and Shopping Lists

*H*aving the proper supplies on hand is vital to surviving storm season. Think of it like an extended sailing trip. The provisions you have when you set sail will have to last you the entire journey, as there is little likelihood of encountering a supermarket on the high seas.

The same concept holds true in the middle of a storm or other crisis situation. Should a major-scale disaster hit, electricity may be disrupted for days or even weeks (see chart, page 6). The ramifications of an extended power outage are difficult to comprehend if you haven't lived through it. Simply stated, there is a whole lot you learn to live without.

The most obvious of these is light. You must either take advantage of daylight hours to prepare meals, or plan for a self-standing, battery-operated light source. Additionally, and perhaps more painfully, all kitchen appliances are rendered defunct. That means no refrigeration for cold storage, which forces you to use nonperishable and shelf-stable items for food preparation, and to manage portions in a way that eliminates or minimizes leftovers. Of course, there is always the option of moving refrigerated foods to a cooler and storing them on ice. However, ice may be scarce before and after a storm, so it's advisable to plan for a worst-case scenario.

A power failure also means the stove, oven, and microwave oven are about as useful as an electric blanket in Equatorial Africa. This simply means preparing meals that require no heat. Actually, this may be a

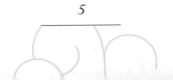

blessing in disguise, as a hot meal is the last thing you will want when the air-conditioning stops working and the humidity levels go through the roof.

Small appliances also are useless. Work around this by stocking your kitchen with basic tools that do not require electricity (see Manual Gadgets, page 24), and by simplifying your recipe repertoire (a soufflé, for example, is out of the question). The recipes contained in *The Storm Gourmet* take all these challenges into account. Every recipe is designed with the worst-case scenario in mind: No single ingredient is dependent on cold storage, and no dish requires temperature cooking. Portions are intentionally kept small, serving two to four people, to minimize leftovers and waste. And every recipe utilizes simple techniques that can be executed without the bells and whistles of a modern kitchen.

Although we've made every effort to minimize waste, some recipes do call for portions of can contents. Which begs the question: What to do with the leftovers? Our advice is to be creative. Ravenous teenagers are always good at making things disappear. Or perhaps the family pet might appreciate a snack. If all else fails, there is always the compost pile.

Storm (year)	Category	Maximum days without power
Charley (2004)	4	13
Ivan (2004)	3	13
Isabel (2003)	2	14
Andrew (1992)	5	37

Source: FPL: Historical Disaster Response by U.S. Electric Utilities [WWW document] www.fpl.com/storm/pdf/hurricane_season_2004.pdf

Given these statistics, you will ideally want to have two weeks' supply of water and food on hand. Many people make the mistake of understocking because of space limitations, cost, or simply because they do not have a plan. Keep in mind the stress of crisis management will increase the need for nutrition and hydration. Nervousness and agitation also will fuel the desire for snacking—especially in children.

Another thing to plan for is the possibility of contaminated city water. Should this happen, you not only will need plenty of drinking water for your family and pets (see Water, page 11), you also will need clean water for personal hygiene, food preparation, and cleanup. You can eliminate much of the cleanup by using paper plates and plastic cups and utensils. This, of course, will lead to more garbage—of which you will have plenty already. In the event of power loss, almost everything in your freezer and refrigerator will have to be discarded (See Appendix I: Refrigerated Foods: To Keep or Not to Keep?). Add to that the disposable dishware, packages, and cans used in food preparation, empty bottles, and the fact that garbage service will likely be disrupted post-storm, and it is obvious why garbage bags are storm-pantry necessities.

The golden rule for disaster provisioning is this: It's important to be organized, have available enough of the right supplies, and to stock up early.

In some cases, such as earthquakes, disaster may strike without warning. Weather events like blizzards and hurricanes are somewhat more predictable, because they have defined seasons. Even then it's difficult to second-guess Mother Nature. For example, August and September are notoriously the most active hurricane months; yet on June 24, 1957, Hurricane Audrey ravaged Louisiana, and on June 19, 1972, Hurricane Agnes wreaked havoc on Florida, Cuba, and portions of the Carolinas. In light of this, the need to plan ahead cannot be overstated.

Starting early also gives you the opportunity to stagger your purchases at comfortable intervals (let's face it, the list can be overwhelming and the grocery bill can add up quickly). Careful planning means bypassing crisis mode and being calmer in the midst of an emergency, when other critical decisions have to be made.

Don't assume you can buy what you need immediately after the storm passes. In the event of a direct hit, power lines will be down and traffic lights will be inoperable. Roads may be flooded, littered with debris, or both. Even a trip to the neighborhood store will not be safe. As for the supermarkets, chances are they will not have electricity either; even if they do, shelves will likely be sparsely populated for many days, as delivery trucks will inevitably be stuck on the wrong side of impassable roads.

In the following pages is a list of items you will need to assemble wholesome and exciting meals for two people (divide or multiply according to the number of persons in your household) for two weeks. To make it easy, we have suggested a fourteen-day meal plan, using recipes from the chapters that follow. Most of these recipes use ingredients that can easily be found at your local super-market. The few specialty ingredients can be sourced at gourmet or ethnic food stores. By adhering to this shopping list, you will be properly armed and ready to execute these menus. The list in no way represents the full gamut of *Storm Gourmet* recipes, so you may want to leaf through the book and find your own favorites. If you wish to vary the recipes or add on to the suggested menus, simply add the appropriate ingredients to the list.

We also include alternative menus for those who wish to go the simpler route and provision for shorter durations, or simply limit their pantry supplies. In the Just the Basics section, you will find a five-day, no-frills meal plan, consisting of our simplest recipes. These recipes use fewer and more common ingredients, many of which are already pantry staples in most homes. While this option provides for basic sustenance, it is just that: basic. You may wish to supplement these meals with snacks of your choice, or your favorite *Storm Gourmet* desserts and appetizers.

One word of advice about ingredients: Levels of quality vary drastically in nonperishables, so buy the best quality you can afford, particularly in prepackaged protein items. Meats and seafood designated as "premium" or "all-white meat" are generally tastier and, in many cases, less processed than the more generic varieties. *Storm Gourmet* recipes use the best quality of available ingredi-ents, including extra-virgin olive oil, organic tahini, balsamic and Chardonnay vinegars, Kalamata olives, and imported preserves. It's only logical that better ingredients will produce a better end product—so choose wisely.

A Fourteen-Day Meal Plan

Day One
Breakfast: Cereal with Milk
Lunch: Bean and Roasted Red Pepper Salad
Dinner: Salmon with Sun-dried Tomatoes and
            Pine Nuts; Chocolate-Vanilla Parfait

Day Two
Breakfast: Peanut Butter Toasts
Lunch: Tropical Tuna Salad
Dinner: Gazpacho "Martinis"; Salade Niçoise

Day Three
Breakfast: Cereal with Milk
Lunch: Savory Ham with Dijon Cream
Dinner: Spicy Salsa; Chipotle Chicken Soft Tacos

Day Four
Breakfast: Fruit Salad; Toast with Jelly
Lunch: Shrimp and White Bean Salad
Dinner: Vichyssoise; Pasta with Salmon in Creamy Dill Sauce

Day Five
Breakfast: Cereal with Milk
Lunch: Curried Chicken
Dinner: Asian Bulgur Pilaf; Rose Water–
scented Pistachio Pudding

Day Six
Breakfast: Peanut Butter Toasts
Lunch: Currant–Mustard Ham
Dinner: Cranberry-Orange Chicken;
Poached Moroccan Fruits

Day Seven
Breakfast: Cereal with Milk
Lunch: Greek-style Bean Salad
Dinner: Tapenade Toasts; Pasta Puttanesca

Day Eight
Breakfast: Fruit Salad; Toast with Jelly
Lunch: Savory Ham with Dijon Cream
Dinner: Salmon with Tahini Sauce; Tiramisu

Day Nine
Breakfast: Cereal with Milk
Lunch: Vichyssoise
Dinner: Mom's Black–eyed–Pea Salad; Honey–
Mustard Chicken with Pecans

Day Ten
Breakfast: Peanut Butter Toasts
Lunch: Bean and Roasted Red Pepper Salad
Dinner: Island Shrimp; Key Lime Pie

Day Eleven
Breakfast: Cereal with Milk
Lunch: Shrimp and White Bean Salad
Dinner: Greek-style Bean Salad; Asian Chicken Pasta Toss

Day Twelve
Breakfast: Fruit Salad; Toast with Jelly
Lunch: Tropical Tuna Salad
Dinner: South of the Border Corn Soup;
            Chipotle Chicken Soft Tacos

Day Thirteen
Breakfast: Cereal with Milk
Lunch: Curried Chicken
Dinner: Hearts of Palm Salad; Lemon Herb Pasta

Day Fourteen
Breakfast: Peanut Butter Toasts
Lunch: Currant–Mustard Ham
Dinner: Salade Niçoise; Poached Moroccan Fruits

Water

The daily requirement of 64 fluid ounces (eight 8-ounce glasses) of water per person is of paramount importance during a crisis, when the body is more stressed and more active. Do not risk dehydration; have plenty of water on hand and drink even if you are not thirsty.

In addition to drinking water, extra water is recommended for food preparation and basic hygiene in the event of sanitation systems failure. If public water becomes contaminated, bottled water will be necessary for everything from brushing your teeth to cleaning plates and cooking utensils to your pet's drinking bowl. Again, the following requirements are for a two–person household:

Minimum drinking-water requirement: 14 gallons
        (1/2 gallon per person per day)
Minimum food preparation/basic sanitation requirement:
        14 gallons (1 gallon per day)
Total water requirement: 28 gallons

Shopping List for the
Ultimate Storm Pantry

Canned Goods

Qty	Size/wt	Item
4	15 oz	Butter beans
1	8 oz	Asparagus tips
2	8 oz	Papaya chunks
3	8 oz	Water chestnuts
1	8 oz	Sweet peas
1	15 oz	Whole cranberry
2	14.5 oz	Cut green beans
2	15 oz	Small red/kidney beans
2	16 oz	Chickpeas (garbanzo beans)
3	15 oz	Wax beans
1	8 oz	Hearts of palm
2	14.5 oz	Sliced potatoes
1	14.5 oz	French green beans
2	10.5 oz	Cream of potato soup
3	10.5 oz	Chicken broth
4	8 oz	Pineapple chunks
2	16 oz	Black-eyed peas
1	14.75 oz	Cream-style sweet corn
1	16 oz	Yams
4	16 oz	Cannellini beans
1	8 oz	Pineapple tidbits
3	15 oz	Fruit salad
1	7.1 oz	Guava nectar
1	8 oz	Artichokes
3	12 oz	Roasted red peppers
1	7 oz	Portobello mushrooms
1	4 oz	Straw mushrooms
1	15 oz	Baby corn
10	8 oz	Table cream*
4	12 oz	Evaporated milk
1	14 oz	Sweetened condensed milk

Nuts and Dried Fruit

Weight	Item
24 oz	Pine nuts
16 oz	Slivered almonds
9.5 oz	Roasted cashews
6 oz	Roasted pistachios
6 oz	Walnuts
6 oz	Pecans
6 oz	Raisins
4 oz	Dried mango
6 oz	Dried cranberries
4 oz	Dried cherries
16 oz	Dates
8 oz	Dried apricots

Condiments, Oils, Pickles, Preserves

Weight	Item
12 oz	Kalamata olives
2 oz	Manzanilla olives
3.5 oz	Capers

12 oz	Dijon mustard
4.1 oz	Imitation bacon bits
5 oz	Soy sauce
16 oz	Raw organic tahini
12 oz	Orange marmalade
12 oz	Red currant preserves
12 oz	Honey
17 oz	Extra-virgin olive oil
5 oz	Sesame oil
17 oz	Balsamic vinegar
16 oz	Apple cider vinegar
12.75 oz	Red wine vinegar
4 oz	Chiles chipotles
11 oz	Orange blossom water
11 oz	Rose water
26 oz	Peanut butter
5 oz	Sun-dried tomatoes
16 oz	Chardonnay vinegar
2 oz	Tabasco
12 oz	Key lime juice

Dry goods and breadstuff

Qty/weight	Item
2 boxes	Breakfast cereal
2 packs	Italian toasts
10	Soft tortillas
1 lb	Powdered milk
4 oz	Instant coffee
2 boxes	Bulgur wheat (tabouli)
12.5 oz	Tortilla chips (corn and blue corn)

Confections

Qty/weight	Item
3.4 oz	Vanilla instant pudding
3.4 oz	Chocolate instant pudding
3.4 oz	Pistachio instant pudding
1 oz	Unflavored gelatin
8 oz	Cocoa
32 oz	Sugar
16 oz	Confectioner's sugar
50 ml	Kahlua coffee liqueur
1	Graham cracker crust
14.4 oz	Graham cracker crumbs
3 oz	Lady fingers

Protein

Qty	Size/Wt	Item
5	7 oz	Pink salmon
4	7 oz	Flaked albacore tuna
9	7 oz	Premium chicken breast
3	10 oz	Chunk lean ham
6	3.53 oz	Premium shrimp
2	6 oz	Light tuna in extra-virgin olive oil

Shelf-stable produce

Qty	Item
4 oz	Ginger
3	Sweet onion
1 head	Garlic
3	Orange
12	Lemons
12	Limes
2	Avocados

Spices, Dried Herbs, Fresh Herbs

We recommend stocking your spice pantry with the spices and dried herbs listed in The Spices of Life, page 18. We also suggest potting and growing fresh herbs, as outlined in Essential Herbs: Potting Your Own Herb Garden. All of these herbs and spices will be useful in executing the recipes in The Storm Gourmet.

*Table Cream

Thick in texture and unsweetened, table cream is a versatile ingredient that can be used in savory dishes or desserts. It is found in the canned milk aisle of most supermarkets.

Instant Pasta

Instant pasta that reconstitutes in room–temperature water is not a commonly found item. In North America, the only manufacturer of such pasta is Pasta U.S.A based in Spokane, Washington. Though they typically supply only the food industry, they will sell their Presto Pasta in bulk to *The Storm Gourmet* readers by mail order. We have tested all their instant pasta varieties and recommend them without reservation.

*(800) 456–2084;
www.pastausa.com/presto_pasta.htm*

When preparing for the storm, don't forget your furry friends. Remember, animals become agitated, just as humans do. Plan ahead for your pets' water and food supplies, and stock up on treats to calm their frazzled nerves.

A Five-Day Plan for Basic Storm Meals
Just the Basics

Day One
Breakfast Cereal with Milk
Lunch Savory Vegetables with Herb Dressing
Dinner Salade Niçoise

Day Two
Breakfast Peanut Butter Toasts
Lunch Vichyssoise
Dinner Creamed Tuna on Toast

Day Three
Breakfast Cereal with Milk
Lunch Dijon Potato Salad
Dinner Honey-Mustard Chicken with Pecans

Day Four
Breakfast Fruit Salad; Toast with Jelly
Lunch Minted Pineapple Ham
Dinner Curried Chicken

Day Five
Breakfast Cereal with Milk
Lunch Savory Ham with Dijon Cream
Dinner Valerie's Tuna Cannellini

Shopping List for the Basic Storm Pantry

Canned Goods

Qty	Size/wt	Item
1	14.5 oz	Cut green beans
1	14.5 oz	French green beans
1	14.5 oz	Baby carrots
1	15 oz	Baby corn
1	16 oz	Chickpeas (garbanzo beans)
2	14.5 oz	Sliced white potatoes
1	14.5 oz	Diced new potatoes
1	10.5 oz	Chicken broth
1	10.5 oz	Cream of potato soup
1	8 oz	Sweet peas
1	8 oz	Chopped mushrooms
1	16 oz	Yams
1	8 oz	Crushed pineapple
1	8 oz	Pineapple tidbits
1	16 oz	Cannellini beans
2	8 oz	Artichoke hearts
1	8 oz	Water chestnuts
1	16 oz	V8® juice
1	15 oz	Fruit salad

Nuts and Dried Fruit

Weight	Item
24 oz	Pine nuts
16 oz	Slivered almonds
6 oz	Pecans
6 oz	Raisins
6 oz	Dried cranberries

Condiments, Oils, Pickles, Preserves

Weight	Item
12 oz	Honey
2 oz	Sliced manzanilla olives
3.5 oz	Capers
12 oz	Dijon mustard
4.1 oz	Imitation bacon bits
5 oz	Soy sauce
12 oz	Kalamata (or black) olives
17 oz	Balsamic vinegar
16 oz	Apple cider vinegar
5 oz	Sun-dried tomatoes
17 oz	Extra-virgin olive oil
12.75 oz	Red wine vinegar
18 oz	Pineapple preserves
26 oz	Peanut butter

Protein

Qty	Size/Wt	Item
4	7 oz	Premium chicken breast
2	10 oz	Chunk lean ham
5	6 oz	Light tuna in extra-virgin olive oil

Shelf-stable Produce

1 head	Garlic
1 medium	Onion
2	Lemons
2	Limes

Spices and Dried Herbs

Oregano
Basil
Red pepper flakes
Salt
Pepper
Curry powder
Parsley flakes
Mint flakes
Chives

The Spices of Life

In the era of exploration, European seamen traveled thousands of nautical miles to the East Indies searching for treasure in the form of spices. In those days, spices were so prized that they were used to measure a man's wealth. During the Middle Ages, a pound of ginger could buy one sheep, and two pounds of mace were traded for a cow. Pepper, the so-called King of Spices, was the currency by which taxes and rents were paid. It is said that a sack of peppercorns was worth a man's life.

There's a reason for that. Spices are to a dish what music is to a party. They liven things up and get noticed. This is particularly important when the luxury of cooking with a full palette of fresh ingredients and a spectrum of flavors simply does not exist. Indeed, this is the very reason our forebears coveted spices: Before refrigeration, food was limited to what was growing in the earth and the livestock that was slaughtered before winter. A pinch of ginger or a sprinkle of pepper and even the lowly parsnip suddenly tasted zesty. Spices bridged the gap between basic sustenance and haute cuisine.

Not unlike the food of the Middle Ages, the basic ingredients for storm cooking are bland. Have you ever tried to eat tuna or green beans right out of a can? Exactly. But add fragrantly spiced sauces, marinades and dressings, and suddenly the entire picture changes. Think of it as a glamour makeover for a plain Jane: You won't believe how good average supermarket ingredients can taste.

Below is a list of the main spices used in *The Storm Gourmet* recipes, along with a brief description of each one's flavor profile. Add them to your storm pantry and instantly up your gastronomy quotient.

Black pepper	A versatile spice, pepper (which comes in whole peppercorns or ground) enhances the flavor of almost any dish. The coarser the grind, the more fiery it is.
Basil	Sweet and fragrant with a slightly nutty taste, basil is used widely in Mediterranean dishes, particularly in vegetable dishes and pasta sauces.
French marjoram	Related to oregano, but sweeter and more delicate in flavor, this herb is perfect for pasta sauces, salad dressings, and vegetables.
Oregano	Used frequently in Greek cuisine, this herb is highly fragrant and pungent, with a slightly minty nose. It is best suited for marinades, salad dressings, meat rubs, fish, and Mediterranean-style sauces.
Salt	Most commonly found in seawater and classified as a mineral, salt is probably the world's most popular flavoring agent. When used sparingly, it adds zest to almost any dish.
Curry powder	Popular in Indian cooking, this blend consists of turmeric, cumin, red pepper, coriander, and other spices.
Parsley	A mild, highly versatile herb that can be used in almost any recipe to bring out the flavor of other herbs.
Mint (spearmint)	A refreshing, versatile herb used to flavor vegetables, fruit, pasta, and some meats (lamb and pork, in particular).
Cinnamon	Sweet, warm, and highly aromatic, cinnamon is commonly used in desserts, but is also a key ingredient in Indian and Moroccan cuisines.
White pepper	A standard peppercorn that has been soaked to remove the black shell. Milder than black pepper, it is used to flavor cream-based soups and sauces.
Paprika	A Hungarian spice available in hot and sweet varieties. Made from ground red peppers, it is used to flavor meats, vegetables, and sauces.
Tamarind paste	Refreshing, fruity, and slightly sour, this exotic spice is often used in curries, chutneys, and Asian dishes as a souring agent.

Sesame	A nutty, earthy seed used as a topping on many Asian, Middle Eastern, and North African dishes. There are black and white varieties, but the flavor is similar.
Vanilla extract	Highly aromatic and sweet, it is used to flavor desserts.
Coriander	Fragrant and slightly citrusy, coriander (comes in flake or powder form) is made from the seeds and leaves of the cilantro plant. In the absence of fresh cilantro, this is a good substitute.
Herbes de Provence	A dried herb blend originating in the Provence region of southern France. The blend may include basil, rosemary, thyme, sage, marjoram, mint, fennel, oregano, and lavender.
Cayenne pepper	This fiery powder comes from the stems and flesh of cayenne chili peppers. It's widely used in Cajun cuisine.

Potting Your Own Herb Garden

*I*f you are one of those people in whose hands potted herbs have suffered an untimely demise, you may think growing herbs is tricky. It's not. If you follow a few basic guidelines, you can have fresh herbs year-round—even in the middle of storm season. We consulted Mary Lambert, Ph.D., a vegetable agent with University of South Florida's Miami–Dade County Extension, for the practical, no-nonsense advice contained in this section.

It is a good idea to begin planning your herb garden a few months before storm season, so that herbs are established and growing. First, set aside the appropriate space. Herbs grow best in pots outdoors, ideally in a screened-in patio or balcony that blocks the wind. Potted herbs can always be brought inside during storms, frost, or high winds.

Start by planting herbs in a soilless medium like a peat-perlite light potting soil. This is fairly standard and is found pre-mixed at most garden centers. Plant in small pots with drainage holes, as too much moisture will lead to root rot. You may want to line the drainage saucer with gravel to provide a protective layer between the plant and sitting water. Gravel is also useful for lining the bottom of the pot. A one-inch layer of gravel will not only help with drainage, it will anchor the plant in windy weather.

Most herbs need plenty of light but not hot, direct sun. Position them in a south- or southeast-facing window so they don't get scorched by the heat. Herbs may be grown indoors with supplemental light. It is possible to augment sunlight with grow lamps (found at most home improvement stores and garden centers) or with a combination of fluorescent and incandescent lights, placed one to two feet above the plants.

Proper nutrition is important. Most people kill plants by overwatering or underwatering, or by overzealous fertilizing. With herbs, less is more. Simply water herbs once a week, or when the surface of the soil is dry. Don't drench; when water starts to seep out the drainage holes, the plant has had enough. Fertilizer should be used sparingly. Part of the reason herbs have such wonderful flavors is that they are a little "stressed." Too much fertilizer detracts from taste. Use small amounts of a slow-release fertilizer (similar to that used for lettuce) as needed.

Below are some specific growing instructions for your *Storm Gourmet* herb garden.*

Mint	A perennial herb, mint is invasive and grows well year-round. Unlike many herbs, it can benefit from cooler temperatures.
Basil	As an annual herb, a basil plant lasts five to six months. When it flowers and sets seed, it is time to start another plant.
Dill	This biennial herb flowers in its second year. Do not consume the flowers. As with basil, start a new plant when it begins to flower.
Parsley	Similar to dill, parsley (available in curly or Italian, which is flat-leaved, varieties) grows for almost two years before flowering and seeding. Replant at the first sign of flowering.
Cilantro	An annual herb, cilantro (coriander) flowers within months of potting. Replant at the first sign of flowering.
Chives	Chives, especially garlic chives, are perennial and hardy. Grow year-round.

While fresh herbs are recommended for The Storm Gourmet *recipes, dried herbs may be substituted. Just keep in mind the flavors will not be as intense. To substitute dried herbs, use half of the fresh-herb requirement (see* Appendix II: Substitutions).

The Backyard Tree
Using Nature's Bounty

S torms are generally not kind to trees. In their storm preparations, most people take the time to prune tree branches, for fear the gales might send them flying through a window. This is particularly true of fruit-laden boughs. Many tropical and subtropical trees, including avocado and mango, are in fruit during hurricane season. If their branches are not cut down, chances are the weight of the fruit will cause them to snap, even in tropical-storm gusts. Either way, it is likely there will be plenty of fallen fruit around—if not in your backyard, surely in your neighbor's. Why let it go to waste?

The Storm Gourmet takes advantage of the most common backyard fruits of the region—oranges, lemons, limes, Key limes, avocados, and mangos, among others. Many recipes utilize the flesh and juice of fresh citrus and tropical and subtropical fruit because nothing compares to the taste of the "real thing." If you live in a city, or have no access to fruit trees, you may wish to purchase some fresh fruit from the supermarket or greengrocer when a storm approaches. These fruits will last for one week to ten days outside the refrigerator.

As a last resort, most of these fruits have dried or canned alternatives, which are noted in APPENDIX II: SUBSTITUTIONS.

Manual Gadgets

*I*f you've lived in a storm-prone area long enough, chances are you've heard (or voiced) this statement: "When the power went out, we realized we had plenty of canned goods—and an electric can opener!"

Modern conveniences may make our lives easier, but they are useless when the power is down. However anachronistic it may seem, manual tools that can be operated without electricity are vital to food preparation during a storm. Remember those old, hand-cranked gadgets from Mom's kitchen? It's time to bring them back. The good news is they are still readily available; most are found in home-goods stores, and even in your supermarket's cooking-implements aisle.

The following tools, categorized by usefulness, are nonelectrical substitutes for the small appliances frequently used in most kitchens. While these are not powerful enough to, say, knead bread dough or pulverize carrots, they are all you will need to execute *The Storm Gourmet* recipes. After all, if it was good enough for Mom . . .

Indispensable Musts

Can opener	Choose a manual style with an ergonomic design, a soft grip, and a good locking system.
Whisk	The wire whisk is a valuable tool for thorough blending and mixing. It works better than a spoon for achieving a smooth consistency and texture.
Screw-top jars	Have several of these, in various sizes, on hand for shaking dressings and sauces.
Martini shaker	In addition to the obvious, it may be used as a makeshift blender for simple soups.
Mortar and pestle	Comes in handy for mashing and crushing everything from spices to garlic.

Useful Extras

Mandolin	A French tool used by professional chefs for precise slicing and julienning. Use in place of a food processor's slicing attachment.
Food chopper	Instead of a food processor, a manual chopper does wonders with onions, nuts, herbs, ginger, and garlic. This simple device, which has a small compartment for food on its base and a hand pump on top, is found in most supermarkets.
Hand beater	Use in place of an electric mixer to blend sauces or add a light, frothy texture to cream toppings.
Manual food processor	Looks like your food processor, but without the cords. Operated completely manually, this implement blends, chops, stirs, whips, slices, and juices.
Potato masher	It may not whip potatoes to that nice, fluffy texture, but it's fine for coarse mashing. Also works well for smashing beans and avocados.

Sample Menus

*I*f you are not in an evacuation zone and are safe to ride the out storm at home, the hours can seem long when you are forced to stay inside, often in the dark, imagining the destruction beyond your shuttered windows. You will probably need things to occupy your (and your little ones') time and divert your attention from the eerie sounds of nature's fury. Even after the storm passes, and your family and home are safe, it will take days or weeks before life is back to normal. Take advantage of that time to slow down, bond with family and friends by preparing meals together, and enjoy the delicious rewards of your foresight and preparation. These menus are designed to create a themed dining experience—a special treat for loved ones and guests. Enjoy!

A Florida–style Brunch
Perfect any day of the week, this midday feast consists of cool and refreshing dishes, which are ideal antidotes to post-storm heat and humidity.
> Avocado Salsa, page 31
> Hearts of Palm Salad, page 41
> Minted Pineapple Ham, page 55
> Island Shrimp, page 66
> Key Lime Pie, page 85
> Spicy Bloody Mary, page 99

A Latin Fiesta
The spicy flavors of Latin American cuisine star in this savory roundup.
> Spicy Salsa, page 32

Tropical Tuna Salad, page 48
South of the Border Corn Soup, page 46
Chipotle Chicken Soft Tacos, page 57
Lemon–Lime Custards, page 83
Mock Sangria, page 95

Picnic for Two

Casual fare doesn't have to be dull. This gourmet picnic is perfect for a lazy lunch or a candlelit cocktail-table dinner.

Tapenade Toasts, page 33
Bean and Roasted Red Pepper Salad, page 44
Curried Chicken, page 56
Currant–Mustard Ham, page 54
Black and Tan Cookies, page 86
Limeade, page 98

A Pan–Asian Supper

Asian and Pacific Rim influences are becoming more and more prevalent on America's tables. This supper is based on the exotic flavors of Asia.

Mango–Carrot Salad, page 50
Chickpea and Potato "Stew", page 60
Asian Bulgur Pilaf, page 58
Peanuty Chicken over Puffed Rice, page 69
Poached Ginger Figs, page 90
Pineapple–Guava Cocktail, page 98

A Mediterranean Sampler

Everyone's favorite! Intensely flavored with a medley of spices and herbs, Mediterranean fare is hearty, comforting and always delicious.

Tomato–Mushroom Bruschetta, page 30
Gazpacho "Martinis", page 42
Salade Niçoise, page 40
Lemon–Herb Pasta, page 64
Tiramisu, page 86
Mock Sangria, page 95

Appetizers

These versatile first courses

are perfect on their own as

snacks, or combined to create

a festive tapas spread.

Tomato–Mushroom Bruschetta

This is a favorite snack in Italy. It's elegant enough to serve your guests, and so easy to prepare that you can whip a batch together in minutes.

> 10–12 Italian toasts
> 14.5 oz (1 can) diced tomatoes, drained
> 4 oz (1 can) chopped mushrooms
> 2 tbsp fresh basil, chopped
> 2 garlic cloves, minced
> 2 tbsp capers
> 2 tbsp extra-virgin olive oil
> salt and pepper

Line up the Italian toasts on a serving plate. In a medium-sized bowl, stir together tomatoes, mushrooms, basil, garlic, capers, and olive oil. Season with salt and pepper to taste. Spoon the mixture on top of the toasts.
10–12 toasts. Serves 4.

Chunky Hummus

This version of the Middle Eastern classic is chunky and full of good flavor.

> 2 cups canned chickpeas, drained and rinsed
> ¼ cup extra-virgin olive oil
> 3 tbsp raw organic tahini
> 3 tbsp fresh lemon juice
> 1 tbsp dried parsley flakes
> 2 garlic cloves, finely minced
> ¼ tsp paprika
> ¼ tsp salt
> ¼ tsp pepper

Place the chickpeas in a medium-sized bowl and squeeze by hand until they reach a thick, pasty consistency. Add olive oil, tahini, lemon juice, parsley, garlic, paprika, salt and pepper, and mash with fork until all ingredients are blended together. The mixture should be chunky but moist (not crumbly). Serve with flatbread or crackers.

Serves 4.

Avocado Salsa

When storms come, avocado branches are the first to snap. Take advantage of all that fruit to create this easy salsa.

    1 small chili pepper
    1 tbsp fresh lime juice
    2 ripe avocados, peeled, pitted, and chopped
    14.5 oz (1 can) petite-diced tomatoes, drained
    1 garlic clove, minced
    ¼ cup fresh cilantro
    salt and pepper
    Tabasco to taste
    tortilla chips

Chop the chili finely into mixing bowl. Add lime juice and avocado flesh. Mash all ingredients with a potato masher until chunky. Squeeze excess liquid from tomatoes. Mash tomatoes, garlic and cilantro into the avocado mixture. Season with salt, pepper and Tabasco to taste. Serve with tortilla chips.

Serves 4.

If wooden spoons, cutting boards, baby pacifiers and bottle nipples, or other porous items come in contact with contaminated water, throw them away. They cannot be safely disinfected.

Spicy Salsa

So fresh tasting and zesty, this is as good as—or better than—the restaurant variety.

>   14.5 oz (1 can) petite–diced tomatoes
>   (with jalapeño, if desired)
>   ⅓ cup sweet onion, minced
>   ¼ tsp salt
>   1 tbsp fresh lime juice
>   ½ cup fresh cilantro, chopped
>   Tabasco
>   tortilla chips

Combine tomatoes, onion, salt, lime juice, and cilantro in a small bowl. Season with Tabasco to taste. Let mixture sit for 1 hour for ingredients to meld. Serve with tortilla chips.
Serves 2-4.

Fruit or vegetable?

There has been much debate as to what a tomato is. Since the eighteenth century, botanists have argued it is a fruit because of the seed content. In the nineteenth century, however, the U.S. Supreme Court ruled it is a vegetable because it is typically served with courses "which constitute the principle part of the repast, and not, like fruit, generally as dessert."

Creamed Tuna in Avocado Boats
(page 35)

Limeade
(*page 98*)

Gazpacho "Martinis"
(*page 42*)

Greek–style Bean Salad
(*page 47*)

Curried Chicken
(*page 56*)

Grapefruit Relish
(*page 76*)

Rose Water–scented Pistachio Pudding
(*page 88*)

Key Lime Pie
(*page 85*)

Tapenade Toasts
(page 33)

Salade Niçoise
(page 40)

Chipotle Chicken Soft Tacos
(page 57)

Valerie's Tuna Cannellini
(page 62)

Tapenade Toasts

A traditional dish from the South of France. We love the chunky texture and puckery flavor of the olives and capers.

12–16 Italian toasts
1 cup Kalamata olives, pitted and chopped
2 tbsp capers
1 cup pine nuts
1 tbsp extra-virgin olive oil
2 tbsp fresh lemon juice
½ tsp dried basil
1 ½ cups fresh parsley
ground black pepper

Using a mortar and pestle, crush pine nuts into a paste. Add the olives, a few at a time, and crush until the olive pieces are very small. Add the capers and parsley, a little at a time, and mash until the mixture has a slightly chunky consistency. Transfer into a bowl. Stir in olive oil, lemon juice, basil, and pepper. Spoon the mixture on top of the toasts.

Serves 4.

Creamy Spinach and Artichoke Dip

Our easy, no-bake version of one of the most popular dips in America.

> 1 cup table cream
> 10.75 oz (1 can) cream of mushroom soup
> 1 cup artichoke hearts, drained and chopped
> 1 cup canned whole–leaf spinach, drained
>   and squeezed of excess liquid
> 1 tsp ground black pepper
> ⅛ tsp cayenne pepper
> pinch herbes de Provence
> ⅛ tsp garlic salt
> 1 tsp fresh lime juice
> tortilla chips

In a medium–sized bowl, combine cream, soup, and lime juice with a wire whisk until well blended. Stir in artichokes and spinach. Season with pepper, cayenne, herbes de Provence and garlic salt. Serve with tortilla chips.
Serves 4.

Thai Peanut Dip

This spicy-sweet sauce is seen on every table in Thailand. The Thai use it for everything, from dipping vegetables to topping stir-fries.

> 3 tbsp chunky peanut butter
> 4 tbsp coconut milk
> 1 tbsp light brown sugar
> 1 tbsp soy sauce
> 1 tbsp fresh lime juice
> ⅛ tsp red pepper flakes

Place all ingredients in a martini shaker and shake vigorously. Serve with breadsticks or rice cakes.
Serves 4.

Creamed Tuna in Avocado Boats

This is so tasty and elegantly presented that no one will believe you threw it together in five minutes. Don't have fresh avocados? Serve this salad on Italian toasts.

6 oz (1 can) light tuna in extra-virgin olive oil, drained
4 tbsp table cream
2 tbsp Dijon mustard
½ cup canned peas
¼ cup fresh parsley, plus more for garnishing
¼ cup canned chopped mushrooms
2 avocados, halved and pitted
cracked black pepper

In a small bowl, combine cream and mustard with a wire whisk until thoroughly blended. Mix in peas, mushrooms, parsley, and tuna. Season with pepper. Spoon mixture into avocado halves. Top with parsley, if desired.
Serves 4.

Pesto and Chickpea Spread

The nutty taste of pesto and the substantial texture of chickpeas is a winning combination.

> 1 cup fresh basil, torn into small pieces
> ¼ cup pine nuts
> 2 cloves garlic, chopped
> 2 tbsp extra-virgin olive oil
> ¼ tsp red pepper flakes
> ½ cup canned chickpeas (garbanzo
>   beans), drained and rinsed
> salt and pepper

Place the chickpeas in a small bowl and squeeze by hand until they reach a thick, pasty consistency. Set aside. Using a mortar and pestle, crush garlic. Add pine nuts, a few at a time, and crush into a paste. Slowly add basil, a little at a time, and crush until basil pieces are very fine. Add red pepper flakes and olive oil, and mash together until mixture has a pasty, oily texture. Transfer basil mixture (pesto) into chickpea paste and stir until well blended. Season with salt and pepper. Serve with Italian toasts, crackers, or breadsticks.
Serves 4.

Storm Gourmet Hurricane Lore

News from Above

In the 1940s, residents of North Carolina's Outer Banks got news about impending hurricanes out of the blue. Planes circled over the most remote regions, dropping containers containing storm warnings onto residents' yards.

Soups and Salads

These recipes make delicious main

courses for lunch or a light supper.

They're perfect for picnics, too!

Salade Niçoise

This hearty salad, served with crusty bread and a glass of white wine, has long been a staple on the sidewalk cafés of the French Riviera.

29 oz (2 cans) sliced white potatoes
12 oz (2 cans) light tuna in extra-virgin olive oil
14.5 oz (1 can) French green beans
1 cup quartered, marinated artichokes
1 tbsp capers
¼ cup black or Kalamata olives, pitted and halved
1 tbsp fresh lemon juice
salt and pepper
anchovies (optional)

For the dressing:

7 tbsp extra-virgin olive oil
3 tbsp red wine vinegar
1 ½ tbsp Dijon mustard
pinch salt
¼ tsp cracked black pepper

Place tuna in a small bowl and toss with the lemon juice. Set aside. Combine potatoes, beans, artichokes, capers, olives, and anchovies in a large salad bowl. Season with salt and pepper and toss together. Add tuna. In a screw-top jar, combine dressing ingredients. Shake vigorously until dressing has a creamy, frothy consistency. Pour dressing over salad and toss.
Serves 4.

Hearts of Palm Salad

In Florida, hearts of palm have been consumed since the pioneer days—and are still considered a local delicacy.

    1 cup canned hearts of palm
    1 cup canned wax beans
    1 cup avocado, cubed
    ¼ cup sun-dried tomatoes, julienned
    3 tbsp pine nuts
    2 tbsp fresh Italian parsley, chopped
    cracked black pepper

For the dressing:
    4 tbsp guava nectar
    2 tbsp apple cider vinegar
    1 tbsp fresh lime juice
    1 tsp sesame oil

Combine hearts of palm, avocado, beans, sun-dried tomatoes, and pine nuts in medium bowl and toss together. In a screw-top jar, combine dressing ingredients and shake well. Pour over salad mixture and toss. Garnish with fresh parsley and top with cracked black pepper.
Serves 4.

Who Wants to Feed a Millionaire?

*H*earts of palm are just what the name suggests: the heart of the sabal palm, Florida's state tree. Once called "swamp cabbage" and considered "poor man's food," these tender hearts were a staple of the local diet. When the state of Florida passed a law to protect the sabal palm, its hearts became scarce and prices went through the roof—hence the delicacy's current nickname, "millionaire's salad."

Mom's Black–eyed–Pea Salad

Ever the resourceful cook, Mom originally threw this salad together from leftovers. It was so good that it instantly became a family favorite.

31.6 oz (2 cans) black–eyed peas, drained and rinsed
1 medium onion, minced
4 tbsp fresh lemon juice
½ cup extra-virgin olive oil
¼ cup fresh parsley
salt
cracked black pepper

Combine peas, onion, and parsley in a medium–sized bowl. Place olive oil and lemon juice in a screw-top jar and shake vigorously, until liquid appears cloudy. Pour over pea mixture and toss. Season with salt and cracked black pepper to taste.
Serves 4.

Gazpacho "Martinis"

Served in martini glasses, this traditional summer soup from Spain's Andalusia region is an elegant first course.

14.5 oz (1 can) petite–diced tomatoes
2 garlic cloves, minced
1 tbsp fresh lemon juice
⅓ cup extra-virgin olive oil
2 tbsp red wine vinegar
½ tsp salt
½ tsp coarsely ground black pepper
1 tbsp dried parsley
½ avocado, peeled, pitted and cubed
Tabasco sauce

Combine tomatoes, garlic, lemon juice, oil, vinegar, parsley, salt and pepper in a martini shaker. Shake vigorously (about 10 seconds).

Pour into martini glasses. Add Tabasco sauce to taste. Garnish with avocado cubes. Serve with breadsticks or flatbread, if desired.
Serves 2.

Vichyssoise

The French have long enjoyed this velvety, cold soup. Don't tell anyone at the Cordon Bleu how easy our version is.

10.5 oz (1 can) cream of potato soup
10.5 oz (1 can) chicken broth
½ cup table cream
2 tbsp onions, minced
½ tsp white pepper
chives, chopped

Place soup and broth in a martini shaker and shake vigorously. Pour into large serving bowl. With a wire whisk, stir in cream until well blended and smooth. Stir in onions and white pepper. Let stand for 1 hour for ingredients to meld. Sprinkle chopped chives before serving.
Serves 4.

*A*ccording to a University of Illinois nutrition study, canned food has plenty of nutritional value. Most vitamin C is retained after canning, even throughout the canned goods' two-year shelf life. Canned poultry and fish have similar levels of protein and vitamins as their fresh and frozen counterparts. Many canned fruits and vegetables are packed with vitamin A and carotene, an important antioxidant. Canned tomatoes contain an important carotenoid called lycopene, which has been touted for its health benefits.

Bean and Roasted Red Pepper Salad

This dish is even better the next day when the vinaigrette has thoroughly marinated the ingredients.

30 oz (2 cans) butter beans, drained and rinsed
1 ½ cups roasted red peppers, sliced
⅓ cup pine nuts
1 large garlic clove, minced
½ cup fresh parsley
¼ cup Kalamata olives, pitted and chopped
salt and pepper

For the dressing:
6 tbsp extra-virgin olive oil
3 tbsp balsamic vinegar
1 tbsp fresh lemon juice

Combine beans, peppers, pine nuts, garlic, parsley and olives in a large bowl. Season with salt and pepper to taste. In a screw-top jar,

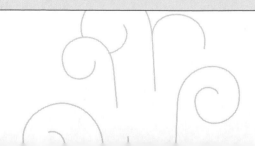

Good to the Last Drop

A product of Modena, Italy, balsamic vinegar was once so prized that aristocratic families included it in the dowries of their daughters and bequeathed it in wills. Some balsamic vinegars are aged in oak casks up to a hundred years. The longer a vinegar ages, the more concentrated, full-bodied and expensive it becomes.

combine dressing ingredients and shake vigorously. Pour dressing over bean mixture and toss well. Let sit 1 hour to overnight before serving.

Serves 4—6.

Dijon Potato Salad

Perfect by itself or as a side dish to just about any main course.

14.5 oz (1 can) diced new potatoes, drained
4 tbsp onion, minced
1 tbsp imitation bacon bits
1 tsp dried parsley flakes
2 tsp capers
salt and pepper
chives, chopped

For the dressing:

4 tbsp extra-virgin olive oil
2 tbsp apple cider vinegar
1 tbsp Dijon mustard

Combine potatoes, onion, bacon bits, parsley, and capers in a medium-sized bowl. Season with salt and pepper to taste. In a screw-top jar, combine dressing ingredients and shake vigorously. Pour dressing over potato mixture and toss well to coat. Top with chopped chives before serving.

Serves 2.

South of the Border Corn Soup

The flavors of Tex-Mex cuisine come together in this hearty soup. Enjoy it as a hearty first course or as a light entrée.

14.75 oz (1 can) cream-style sweet corn
10.5 oz (1 can) chicken broth
1 cup table cream
½ tsp white pepper
1 tbsp fresh lime juice
1 cup black beans, drained and rinsed
½ cup roasted red peppers, chopped
¼ cup fresh cilantro, chopped
Tabasco
blue tortilla chips, broken

Place corn and broth in martini shaker and shake vigorously. Pour into large bowl. Stir in cream with wire whisk until well blended. Stir in beans, peppers, cilantro, and lime. Season with pepper and Tabasco to taste. Let sit 1 hour so ingredients can meld. Top with tortilla chips before serving.
Serves 4.

Greek-style Bean Salad

If you love beans, this lemony, zesty dish is for you.

⅔ cup canned cut green beans, drained
⅔ cup canned small red or kidney
    beans, drained and rinsed
⅔ cup canned garbanzo beans, drained and rinsed
⅔ cup canned wax beans, drained
⅔ cup canned cannellini beans, drained and rinsed
1 ½ tsp dried oregano
½ cup sweet onion, minced
½ tsp salt
½ tsp cracked black pepper
½ cup fresh parsley, chopped
¼ cup extra-virgin olive oil
¼ cup fresh lemon juice

In a large bowl, combine beans, onion, parsley, salt and pepper. In small bowl or cup, whisk oil, lemon, and oregano until well blended (mixture should appear cloudy). Pour over bean mixture and toss. *Serves 4.*

Tropical Tuna Salad

Tuna gets paired up with tropical fruit in this light, summery salad.

1 ½ cups flaked albacore tuna
½ cup canned diced pineapple
½ cup canned papaya chunks
2 tbsp slivered almonds
2 tbsp dried mango, chopped
1 tsp ground black pepper
1 tbsp fresh Italian parsley, chopped

For the dressing:

6 tbsp extra-virgin olive oil
3 tbsp balsamic vinegar
1 tbsp Dijon mustard
1 tsp salt

Any Way You Slice It

Mango, which originated in India and now grows prolifically in south Florida and other subtropical zones, can be frustratingly difficult to handle. In fact, the peeling process is such a messy business that it is sometimes referred to as "the mango tango." Most people cut the fruit in half lengthwise, bypassing the flat pit, and cut the flesh diagonally to produce small cubes. Others peel the fruit with a vegetable peeler, cut the flesh away from the pit, and slice. The flesh sticks to the pit, and removing it deftly does take a bit of practice—but mango is its own reward.

In a screw-top jar, combine oil, vinegar, salt and mustard, and shake vigorously. In a medium bowl, combine tuna, fruit and almonds. Pour dressing over tuna mixture and toss. Top with pepper and parsley.

Serves 4.

Shrimp and White Bean Salad

Chardonnay vinegar adds a hint of Wine Country earthiness to this simple salad.

  7 oz (2 packages) premium shrimp
  1 cup canned white or cannellini beans
  ½ tsp herbes de Provence
  ½ tsp oregano
  salt
  cracked black pepper
  ½ cup fresh parsley, chopped

For the dressing:

  1 tbsp fresh lemon juice
  6 tbsp extra-virgin olive oil
  3 tbsp Chardonnay vinegar

Combine shrimp, beans, herbes de Provence, oregano, and parsley in medium-sized bowl. Season with salt and pepper to taste. In a screw-top jar, combine dressing ingredients and shake vigorously. Pour dressing over shrimp mixture and toss well.

Serves 2.

Mango-Carrot Salad

This Asian-inspired dish is so fruity and perfumed that some people enjoy it as a dessert.

1 small mango, peeled, pitted and cut into thin slices
14.5 oz (1 can) sliced carrots
½ cup slivered almonds
fresh chives, chopped

For the dressing:
2 tbsp fresh-squeezed orange juice
1 tbsp fresh lime juice
1 tbsp honey
1 tsp orange-blossom water
1 tsp sesame oil
1 ½ tsp sesame seeds

Combine mango, carrots, and almonds in a medium-sized bowl. In a screw-top jar, combine dressing ingredients and shake vigorously, ensuring honey is fully incorporated. Pour dressing over carrot-mango mixture and toss well to coat. Sprinkle with chopped chives before serving.
Serves 2-4.

Storm Gourmet Hurricane Lore

Equal
Opportunity

Before the hurricane and tropical storm naming system was officially accepted, storms were named for the areas they ravaged (Hurricane San Felipe of 1876), the ships they wrecked (The Racer Storm of 1837), or the holiday during which they unleashed their fury (Labor Day Hurricane of 1935). When the official naming system went into effect in the 1950s, storms were given women's names—supposedly for certain women's tempestuous tempers. That lasted until 1979, when women protested this discrimination. Women's groups petitioned the World Meteorological Organization and succeeded in adding men's names to the naming system.

Main Courses

Hearty, satisfying and surprisingly

simple, these anytime meals

are wholesome solutions for

storm season—and perfect for

busy lives year-round.

Savory Ham with Dijon Cream

This easy ham salad will become a fast favorite.

> 10 oz (1 can) chunk lean ham, drained and cubed
> 1 cup table cream
> ¼ cup Dijon mustard
> 1 cup sliced manzanilla olives
> 2 tbsp sun-dried tomatoes, julienned
> 1 tbsp imitation bacon bits
> 2 tbsp pine nuts
> 1 tsp dried parsley flakes
> cracked black pepper

Combine cream and mustard in a small bowl. Stir with wire whisk until smooth and thoroughly blended. Add ham, olives, tomatoes, pine nuts, bacon bits, and parsley flakes. Toss well to coat. Season with cracked black pepper.
Serves 2.

Currant–Mustard Ham

This unbelievably easy recipe takes five minutes to prepare and tastes surprisingly delicious.

> ½ cup red currant preserves
> 4 tbsp Dijon mustard
> 10 oz (1 can) chunk lean ham, drained and cubed

Stir together preserves and mustard with wire whisk until well blended. Add ham and toss to coat.
Serves 2.

Minted Pineapple Ham

Savory ham gets a tropical twist in this tasty luncheon favorite.

10 oz (1 can) chunk lean ham, drained and cubed
½ cup pineapple preserves
4 tbsp canned crushed pineapple, juice reserved
1 tbsp pineapple juice
2 tbsp fresh lime juice
1 tbsp fresh mint, minced
cracked black pepper

In a medium bowl, stir together preserves, pineapple, juices and mint until well blended. Add ham and toss to coat. Season with cracked black pepper to taste.
Serves 2.

If the weatherman announces a storm warning, place some water bottles in the freezer. If there is a power outage, the frozen water will eventually melt so you can drink it ice-cold—a huge benefit when the air-conditioning is not working. The frozen bottles can also be used as an ice substitute in the freezer or in coolers. Store the rest of your water supply in a cool, dark place; the liquid will be just below room temperature.

Curried Chicken

Curry spices and raisins add a fragrant, exotic twist to everyday chicken salad.

14 oz (2 packages) premium chicken breast, drained
½ cup canned sliced water chestnuts, drained
⅔ cup canned pineapple tidbits, drained
2 tbsp raisins
⅓ cup slivered almonds
1 ½ tsp curry powder
1 tbsp fresh lemon juice
1 tsp soy sauce
2 tbsp table cream
pepper

Place chicken, pineapple, water chestnuts, raisins, and almonds in a medium-sized bowl and toss together. Season with pepper. In a screw-top jar, combine cream, lemon juice, soy sauce, and curry powder, and shake vigorously.* Pour over chicken mixture and toss to coat.
Serves 2.

* Dressing ingredient measurements may be doubled if you prefer a creamier salad.

Cranberry-Orange Chicken

This dish makes us think of Thanksgiving. We made it after Hurricane Jeanne to give thanks that our house was still standing!

7 oz (1 package) premium chicken breast, drained
1 orange
15 oz (1 can) whole cranberry
2 tbsp honey
2 tbsp fresh lemon juice

2 tbsp orange-blossom water
2 tbsp walnuts

Peel orange and remove white membrane, reserving peel. Section flesh and dice. Place into a large bowl. Mince half of the peel finely, and add to bowl. Add chicken, cranberry, and walnuts. In a screw-top jar, combine orange-blossom water, lemon juice, and honey, and shake well. Pour over mixture and blend well. Let sit for 30 minutes, to allow ingredients to meld.
Serves 2.

Chipotle Chicken Soft Tacos

If you have guests coming, make a big batch of this and let people build their own tacos. It's a super crowd-pleaser.

7 oz (1 package) premium chicken breast, drained
1 cup canned diced new potatoes, drained
½ cup canned sweet corn, drained
2 tbsp sweet onion, minced
1 ripe avocado, peeled, pitted and diced
2 to 4 chiles chipotles, depending on taste
3 tbsp fresh lime juice
⅓ cup fresh cilantro, chopped
¼ cup apple cider vinegar
salt and pepper
soft tortillas

Combine chicken, potatoes, corn, chipotles, and onion in a medium-sized bowl. In a screw-top jar, combine vinegar, lime juice, salt, and cilantro, and shake vigorously. Pour over chicken mixture and toss. Season with pepper. Let sit for 30 minutes to allow ingredients to meld. Mix in avocado before serving. Place in soft tortillas and fold.
Serves 2—4.

Asian Bulgur Pilaf

Cashews add a wonderful, nutty flavor and texture to this light Asian dish.

1 box (10 oz) bulgur wheat (tabouli)
7 oz (1 can) portobello mushrooms, drained
1 cup baby corn
1 tbsp fresh ginger, minced
¾ cup canned sweet peas
¼ cup roasted cashews, chopped coarsely
ground black pepper
fresh parsley, chopped

For the dressing:
¼ cup soy sauce
1 tsp honey
2 tbsp fresh lemon juice
2 tsp sesame oil
1 tbsp black sesame seeds

Prepare bulgur wheat according to package instructions, using room temperature water. When the wheat has absorbed all the liquid, fluff with fork. Add corn, mushrooms, ginger, and peas. Season with pepper and toss. In a screw-top jar, combine dressing ingredients and shake well. Pour over pilaf and toss together. Garnish with parsley and cashews.
Serves 2.

Honey–Mustard Chicken with Pecans

This rich sauce is inspired by the tastes of the South. Some people like to substitute dried figs for cranberries for an even heartier flavor.

14 oz (2 packages) premium chicken breast, drained
½ cup Dijon mustard
¼ cup honey
2 tbsp extra–virgin olive oil
½ cup pecans, chopped
2 tbsp yam syrup
2 cups canned yams, sliced, syrup reserved
2 tbsp dried cranberries

Place yams, chicken, and pecans in medium bowl. In large screw–top jar, combine mustard, honey, oil, and syrup and shake vigorously. Pour over chicken mixture and toss. Before serving, top with dried cranberries.
Serves 2–4.

Canned foods have use-by dates, but not expiration dates. Because of the high-heat process used in canning, these foods are safe even if kept on a shelf for long periods of time. Generally, canned goods should be consumed within two years of purchase to avoid changes in texture or taste quality.

Chickpea and Potato "Stew"

This Indian-style vegetarian bowl is a satisfying anytime snack. Tamarind paste is found in most Asian groceries.

14.5 oz (1 can) chickpeas, drained and rinsed
14.5 oz (1 can) diced new potatoes, drained
1 small onion, diced
2 tbsp tamarind paste
6 tbsp water
1 tsp cumin powder
½ tsp cayenne pepper
salt and pepper
2 tbsp fresh cilantro, chopped

Combine chickpeas, potatoes and onions in a medium-sized bowl. Season with salt and pepper and toss. Mix the tamarind paste and water in a small bowl until paste is completely dissolved. Add the cumin and cayenne to the tamarind mixture. Pour over the bean-potato mixture and toss well to coat. Garnish with fresh cilantro before serving.
Serves 2.

Miracle Beans

Chickpeas, also known as garbanzo beans, have long been prized for their aphrodisiac qualities. Desert dwellers believed that great quantities of chickpeas, washed down with honey-spiked camel's milk, increased the sexual prowess. The Flemish botanist Dodonaeus also touted chickpeas' libido-boosting qualities, insisting they should be avoided by scholars and priests.

Salmon–Tabouli Salad with Sun–dried Tomatoes and Pine Nuts

Not everyone realizes tabouli is an instant food. In this dish, it is an excellent foil for the rich texture of salmon and the puckery Dijon vinaigrette.

1 box (10 oz) bulgur wheat (tabouli)
14 oz (2 cans) premium pink salmon, drained
3 tbsp pine nuts
1 cup canned asparagus tips
¼ cup sun–dried tomatoes, julienned
¼ tsp salt
1 tbsp fresh lemon juice
2 tbsp fresh parsley, chopped
pepper

For the dressing:
6 tbsp extra–virgin olive oil
3 tbsp red wine vinegar
1 tbsp Dijon mustard

In a medium–sized bowl, prepare bulgur wheat according to package instructions, using room–temperature water. When the wheat has absorbed all the liquid, fluff with fork. In a separate bowl, toss salmon with lemon juice, salt and pepper and set aside. Add pine nuts, asparagus, sun–dried tomatoes, parsley, and salmon to the bulgur wheat. Toss all ingredients together. In a screw–top jar, combine dressing ingredients and shake well. Pour over wheat salad and toss. Serve with flatbread crackers, if desired.
Serves 4.

Salmon with Tahini Sauce

Tahini, the classic sesame paste, has been a Mediterranean and Middle Eastern staple for centuries. We use raw organic tahini because of its pure sesame flavor.

7 oz (1 can) premium pink salmon, drained
4 tbsp fresh lemon juice
⅔ cup raw organic tahini
2 garlic cloves, minced
2 tbsp fresh parsley, chopped
1 tsp black sesame seeds
salt and pepper

Combine lemon and garlic in a small bowl. Gradually add tahini, blending with hand blender until smooth. Stir in parsley and salmon. Season with salt and pepper to taste. Sprinkle with sesame seeds before serving.
Serves 2.

Valerie's Tuna Cannellini

An herbalist friend whispered this recipe to us. The fresh herbs make all the difference here.

12 oz (2 cans) light tuna in extra-virgin olive oil, drained
2 cups canned cannellini beans, drained and rinsed
2 tbsp capers
1 cup artichoke hearts, drained and chopped
½ tsp red pepper flakes
½ cup fresh parsley, chopped
½ cup fresh basil, chopped
¼ cup extra-virgin olive oil
1 ½ tbsp balsamic vinegar
ground black pepper

Combine tuna, beans, capers, artichoke hearts, red pepper, parsley, and basil in a medium-sized bowl. Combine olive oil and vinegar in screw-top jar and shake well. Pour over tuna mixture and toss. Season with pepper to taste.
Serves 4.

Asian Chicken Pasta Toss

The fresh, clean taste of this pasta dish makes it a warm-weather favorite.

6 oz instant pasta
7 oz (1 package) premium chicken breast, drained
½ cup canned straw mushrooms
1 tbsp fresh ginger, minced
¼ cup fresh cilantro, chopped
¼ cup soy sauce
1 tbsp fresh lemon juice
1 tbsp fresh lime juice
1 tbsp sesame seeds
1 tsp sesame oil
cracked black pepper

Cover pasta in water and reconstitute until al dente, approximately 15 minutes. Drain pasta. Place chicken, ginger, mushrooms, and cilantro in a large pasta bowl. In a small bowl or cup, combine soy sauce, oil, lemon, lime, and sesame seeds with a wire whisk until well blended. Pour over chicken mixture and toss well. Top with cracked black pepper to taste. Add pasta and toss.
Serves 2.

Provençal Chicken Pasta

The classic tomato sauce of Provence, in its no-cook manifestation.

2 cups instant pasta
7 oz (1 package) premium chicken breast, drained
14.5 oz (1 can) diced tomatoes
⅓ cup onion, finely chopped
2 garlic cloves, minced
1 tbsp extra-virgin olive oil
4 oz (1 can) chopped mushrooms
1 tbsp fresh basil, chopped
2 tbsp fresh parsley, chopped
½ tsp dried French marjoram
½ tsp dried oregano
salt and pepper

Cover pasta with water and reconstitute until al dente, approximately 15 minutes. Drain pasta and place in a serving bowl. In a small bowl, combine the chicken, olive oil, and a pinch each of marjoram and oregano. Toss and set aside. In a medium-sized bowl, combine tomatoes, onion, garlic, mushrooms, fresh herbs, and the remaining marjoram and oregano. Stir together until well blended. Season with salt and pepper to taste. Add the chicken and toss well to coat. Spoon sauce over pasta and serve.
Serves 2.

Lemon-Herb Pasta

This light, summery dish is packed with flavor, compliments of the fresh herbs.

10 oz instant pasta
2 tbsp fresh basil, chopped
1 cup fresh parsley, chopped
2 tbsp fresh mint, chopped
2 tbsp fresh dill, chopped
2 tbsp pine nuts
½ tsp cracked black pepper

¼ tsp salt
¼ tsp dried French marjoram
4 tbsp extra-virgin olive oil
4 tbsp lemon juice

Cover pasta with water and reconstitute until al dente, approximately 15 minutes. Drain pasta and place in serving bowl. Top with fresh herbs and pine nuts. Season with salt, pepper, and marjoram and toss. In a small cup or bowl, combine oil and lemon juice and whisk vigorously until well blended (mixture should appear cloudy). Pour over pasta and toss.
Serves 2.

Pasta with Salmon in Creamy Dill Sauce

Hearty and satisfying!

10 oz instant pasta
14 oz (2 cans) premium pink salmon, drained
1 cup table cream
2 tbsp fresh lemon juice
2 tbsp evaporated milk
2 tbsp fresh dill, chopped, plus more for garnishing
½ tsp salt
½ tsp sugar
cracked black pepper

Cover pasta with water and reconstitute until al dente, approximately 15 minutes. Drain and place in serving bowl. In a medium-sized bowl, combine cream, milk, lemon juice, dill, salt, and sugar with wire whisk until thoroughly blended. Stir in salmon until coated. Spoon sauce over pasta. Season with cracked black pepper and garnish with dill.
Serves 4.

Island Shrimp

For this recipe, we use organic, thick-cut Seville orange marmalade. Its bitter-sweet flavor and chunky texture provide a wonderful, aromatic base.

> 7 oz (2 packages) premium shrimp
> ¼ cup thick-cut orange marmalade
> 1 ½ tsp fresh ginger, minced
> 2 tbsp fresh lemon juice
> 1 tsp fresh mint, minced
> ¼ cup canned water chestnuts, drained
> ¼ cup canned pineapple chunks, drained
> 1 tbsp dried mango, chopped

In a medium-sized bowl, combine marmalade, ginger, lemon juice, and mint and stir until well blended. Add shrimp and toss to coat. Let marinate for at least 30 minutes. Add mango, water chestnuts, and pineapple to the mixture. Toss and serve.
Serves 2.

The Cart before the Horse

Believe it or not, the can opener was invented forty-eight years after the advent of the can. The early cans, invented by Londoner Peter Durand in 1810, had to be opened using a hammer and chisel. The can opener was introduced in 1858 by Ezra Warner of Waterbury, Connecticut.

Pasta Puttanesca

In the brothels of Old Rome, the ladies of the night cooked this pasta to entice passersby. Even the storm version is full of fragrant herbs and lusty textures.

2 cups instant pasta
14.5 oz (1 can) diced tomatoes
3 filets anchovies, finely chopped
3 cloves garlic, minced
½ cup Kalamata olives, pitted and chopped
¼ cup capers
1 tbsp extra-virgin olive oil
2 tbsp fresh basil, chopped
½ tsp red pepper flakes
½ tsp dried oregano
½ tsp cracked black pepper
pinch salt

Cover pasta with water and reconstitute until al dente, approximately 15 minutes. Drain pasta and place in large serving bowl. In a separate bowl, combine all other ingredients and stir together until well blended. Let sit 1 hour to allow ingredients to meld. Spoon sauce over pasta and serve.
Serves 4.

Savory Vegetables in Herb Dressing

Vegetarians love this recipe. It may be served as a light main course or as a side dish in lieu of a salad.

1 cup canned green beans, drained
1 cup canned baby carrots, drained
1 cup whole baby corn, drained
1 cup canned garbanzo beans, drained and rinsed
2 tbsp fresh mint, chopped
2 tbsp Italian parsley, chopped

For the dressing:

¼ cup vegetable juice (like V8®)
¼ cup red wine vinegar
1 clove garlic, minced
pinch of dried oregano
pinch of dried basil
¼ tsp red pepper flakes
salt and pepper

Combine beans, carrots, corn, parsley, and mint in medium-sized bowl. In a screw-top jar, combine dressing ingredients and shake vigorously. Pour over vegetables and toss well.
Serves 4.

Peanuty Chicken over Puffed Rice

Puffed rice? It sounds crazy, but its crispy texture is the perfect complement to the rich peanut sauce.

12.5 oz (1 can) premium chicken breast
8 tbsp creamy peanut butter
¼ tsp chili oil
1 cup coconut milk
1 tsp dark soy sauce
2 tsp light brown sugar
2 tbsp fresh cilantro, chopped
cracked black pepper
2 cups puffed rice cereal

In a martini shaker, combine peanut butter, coconut milk, soy sauce, chili oil, and brown sugar. Shake vigorously until all ingredients are combined, ensuring peanut butter is thoroughly incorporated. Place chicken in a medium–sized bowl. Top with peanut sauce and toss to coat. Spoon chicken mixture over puffed rice cereal. Garnish with fresh cilantro and season with cracked black pepper. Serve immediately.
Serves 2–4.

*B*ecause hurricanes are often accompanied by tidal surges, the public water supply may become contaminated. Be sure to listen to television or radio reports for the latest updates on water safety.

Pasta with Pesto Sauce

This traditional Italian pesto is made the old-fashioned way—using a mortar and pestle.

> 2 cups instant pasta
> 2 cups fresh basil, minced
> ¼ cup pine nuts
> 2 cloves garlic, minced
> 3 tbsp extra–virgin olive oil
> ¼ tsp red pepper flakes
> salt
> cracked black pepper

Cover pasta with water and reconstitute until al dente, approximately 15 minutes. Drain pasta and place in a serving bowl. Using a mortar and pestle, thoroughly crush garlic. Add pine nuts, a few at a time, and crush into a paste. Slowly add basil, a little at a time, and crush until basil pieces are very fine. Add red pepper flakes and olive oil, and mash together until mixture has a pasty, oily texture. Spoon pesto over pasta. Season with salt and pepper to taste. Toss until pasta is lightly covered with the pesto, and serve.
Serves 4.

Storm Gourmet Hurricane Lore
The Shark Oil Prophecy

Prior to the advent of the aircraft reconnaissance system, locals used all manner of prediction systems. In Bermuda, folks put more stake in the shark oil than in the weatherman. The oil from the liver of the puppy shark is bottled and hung outside. Bermudan lore says the oil, which is normally clear, turns milky white when a hurricane is approaching.

Dressings and Sauces

These recipes are a snap to
prepare, and flexible enough
to use with a myriad of dishes.
Experimenting is encouraged!

Tahini Dressing

The nutty taste of tahini (sesame paste) makes this dressing an ideal complement to vegetables and fish.

     2 tbsp raw organic tahini
     2 tbsp apple cider vinegar
     2 tbsp sherry
     2 tbsp sesame oil
     1 tbsp soy sauce
     1 garlic clove, minced

In a small bowl, combine vinegar, sherry, oil, soy sauce, and garlic with a wire whisk until well blended. Using the hand blender, incorporate the tahini, a little at a time, into the mix. Blend until smooth and creamy.
Serves 2–4.

Apple and Cider Vinegar Dressing

The sweet-tart combination of apple and mustard makes for a refreshing salad and vegetable topping.

     2 tbsp sunflower oil
     2 tbsp concentrated apple juice
     2 tbsp apple cider vinegar
     1 tbsp Dijon mustard
     1 garlic clove, crushed
     salt and pepper

Place all ingredients in a screw–top jar and shake vigorously until well blended.
Serves 2–4.

Asian Peanut Sauce

This nutty, rich sauce is excellent by itself or as an accompaniment for chicken.

> 8 tbsp creamy peanut butter
> ¼ tsp chili oil
> 1 cup coconut milk
> 1 tsp dark soy sauce
> 2 tsp light brown sugar
> 1 tsp dried cilantro flakes
> cracked black pepper

Combine all ingredients in a martini shaker and shake vigorously, ensuring peanut butter is completely incorporated. Sauce is ready when the mixture is light brown, smooth, and creamy.
Serves 4.

Mustard Maple Vinaigrette

This Southern classic may be used to top everything from pasta to fried green tomatoes.

> 4 tbsp extra-virgin olive oil
> 1 tbsp balsamic vinegar
> 1 tbsp maple syrup (or honey)
> 1 tbsp Dijon mustard
> cracked black pepper

Combine all ingredients in a screw-top jar and shake vigorously until well blended, ensuring syrup is fully incorporated.
Serves 2–4.

Grapefruit Relish

Plenty of grapefruit in your backyard? Use it to create this tangy relish, a refreshing side dish to just about anything.

   1 grapefruit, peeled, white pith removed, and sectioned
   1 tbsp fresh mint, chopped
   1 tbsp guava nectar
   1 tbsp fresh lemon juice
   1 tsp fresh ginger, peeled and minced
   1 tsp lemon zest

Combine all ingredients in a small bowl and toss. Let sit 1 hour to allow ingredients to meld.
Serves 2–4.

First to Safety

If you like grapefruit, thank the French. In 1823, globetrotting French Count Odette Philippe brought the first grapefruit trees from the Bahamas to Safety Harbor in Tampa Bay, Florida.

Walnut Raspberry Vinaigrette

Even the simplest salads become elegant with this fragrant dressing.

2 tbsp raspberry vinegar
1 tsp raspberry preserves
1 tbsp walnuts, chopped
3 tbsp walnut oil
3 tbsp extra-virgin olive oil
salt and pepper

Using a mortar and pestle, crush the nuts into very small pieces. Place nuts, oils, vinegar, and preserves into screw-top jar and shake vigorously. Season with salt and pepper to taste.
Serves 2–4.

Classic Dijon Vinaigrette

A European café classic, this dressing has become a favorite the world over. Some people add crushed garlic to this recipe for a little extra zing.

7 tbsp extra-virgin olive oil
3 tbsp red wine vinegar
1 ½ tbsp Dijon mustard
pinch salt
¼ tsp cracked black pepper

Place all ingredients in screw-top jar and shake vigorously until well blended.
Serves 2–4.

Guava Vinaigrette

Guava has become a staple in Florida cuisine. This dressing works especially well on fish-based salads.

4 tbsp guava nectar
2 tbsp apple cider vinegar
1 tbsp fresh lime juice
1 tsp sesame oil

Place all ingredients in screw-top jar and shake vigorously until well blended.
Serves 2–4.

Storm Gourmet Hurricane Lore
Earth Watch

*J*ust as every dark cloud has a silver lining, hurricanes can actually be good for the earth. According to studies, hurricanes prevent heat from building up unchecked on the ocean waters, thus sustaining the right temperatures for the survival of marine life. Hurricanes also help circulate greenhouse gases and prevent the ocean from leaching large amounts of carbon dioxide from the atmosphere.

Desserts

*Sweets make wonderful treats, and
are especially comforting in a time
of crisis. With these simple recipes,
the entire family can get involved.
They are so easy to prepare, even
the little ones can make them.*

Poached Moroccan Fruits

Dried fruits are staples of the North African diet. Perfumed with fragrant spices and orange-blossom water, this dish evokes images of exotic lands.

1 cup dates, pitted and julienned
1 orange, peeled, white pith removed, and sectioned
½ cup dried apricots, julienned
3 tbsp dried cherries
3 tbsp slivered almonds
1 tsp sugar
1 tsp cinnamon
½ cup orange-blossom water
2 tbsp fresh lemon juice
2 tbsp honey

Place dried fruits, orange sections and almonds in a small bowl. Sprinkle sugar and cinnamon over fruit mixture and toss well to coat. In a small cup or bowl, combine orange-blossom water, lemon juice, and honey with a wire whisk until thoroughly blended. Pour over the fruit and toss. Let marinate for 15–20 minutes before serving.
Serves 4.

Black Forest Tarts

This instant version of the beloved cake is sweet and satisfying.

3.4 oz (1 box) chocolate instant pudding
1 ½ cup (1 can) evaporated milk
½ cup water
6–8 chocolate cookies, crushed
1 cup dried cherries
½ cup sweetened coconut
½ cup chopped walnuts
2 tbsp grated dark chocolate

Combine milk and water in a medium-sized bowl. Add instant pudding and stir with a wire whisk until mixture is well blended and begins to thicken. Line dessert bowls with chocolate cookie crumbs. Spoon two tablespoons of pudding into each bowl. Layer the cherries next, then the coconut, dividing equally among the bowls. Spoon the remainder of the pudding into each bowl. Top with walnuts and grated chocolate. Let set for 1 hour before serving.
Serves 4.

Lemon-Lime Custards

These sweet-tart custards get their essence from fresh lemons and limes—substitutions are discouraged in this case.

¼ cup sugar
2 tbsp fresh lemon juice
2 tbsp fresh lime juice
zest of 1 lemon, grated
zest of 1 lime, grated
¼ cup Marsala wine
1 cup table cream
½ cup graham cracker crumbs

Combine juices, zests, sugar, and Marsala in a small bowl. Let sit for 1 hour to allow ingredients to meld. Add the cream and blend with a wire whisk until smooth. Line dessert glasses with graham cracker crumbs. Spoon custard on top of the crumbs. Garnish with lime zest, if desired.
Serves 4.

Chocolate–Vanilla Parfait

Everybody loves parfait! A snap to make and so good they'll want seconds.

    3.4 oz (1 box) vanilla instant pudding
    3.4 oz (1 box) chocolate instant pudding
    3 cups (2 cans) evaporated milk
    1 cup water
    8 tbsp graham cracker crumbs
    4 tbsp slivered almonds
    1 tbsp dried cherries for garnish

Combine 1 ½ cups of milk and ½ cup water in a medium-sized bowl. Add vanilla pudding and stir with a wire whisk until mixture is well blended and begins to thicken. Combine the remaining milk and water in a separate bowl, and repeat the process with the chocolate pudding. Line parfait glasses with 1 tbsp each graham cracker crumbs. Spoon the vanilla pudding into each glass, dividing evenly. Next, layer the remaining graham cracker crumbs and the almonds, dividing evenly among the glasses. Top with chocolate pudding. Garnish with dried cherries. Let set for 1 hour before serving.
Serves 4.

Key Lime Pie

There are hundreds of versions of this Florida Keys classic. This one is a traditional recipe, tweaked for the storm kitchen.

1 9-inch graham cracker crust
14 oz (1 can) sweetened condensed milk
¼ cup Key lime juice, fresh if available
¼ cup fresh lemon juice
1 tsp unflavored gelatin
1 cup table cream
grated lime rind

Combine lime and lemon juices. Sprinkle gelatin into lime mix and stir well until gelatin is completely dissolved. Stir the mixture into the milk with a wire whisk until well blended. Stir table cream to ensure it is smooth and consistent. Fold cream into lime–milk mixture, and pour into crust. Sprinkle grated lime rind on top, if desired. Let stand at least 1 hour to thicken.
Serves 6—8.

The Great Debate

The true origin of Key lime pie is a subject of heated debate in Florida. Graham cracker crust or pastry crust? Green or pale yellow? Meringue or no? While all versions (and there are many) are delicious, the original Key lime pie originated in the 1850s. The early Florida Keys bakers insisted on a pastry crust with a meringue—not whipped cream—topping. Repeated power outages due to hurricanes led to the popularity of the graham cracker crust—no baking needed!

Tiramisu

The name means "pick me up" in Italian—probably because of the quantity of coffee and sugar.

4 tbsp instant coffee
4 tbsp sugar
12 oz water
2 tbsp Kahlua coffee liqueur
3 oz (approximately 25) ladyfingers
2 cups table cream
¾ cup unsifted confectioners sugar
1 ½ tsp vanilla extract
¼ cup cocoa powder, sifted
¼ cup confectioners sugar, sifted

In a martini shaker, combine sugar, water, and coffee and shake vigorously. Taste mixture to ensure it is strong and sweet. Add Kahlua and stir. Pour into spouted container, omitting froth. Line the bottom of a 9 x 9 pan with ladyfingers in a tight arrangement (ladyfingers should be touching, but not overlapping, each other). Pour coffee mixture over ladyfingers, taking care to soak each completely. In a bowl, combine cream and vanilla until blended. With a wire whisk, stir in sugar gradually until mixture is smooth. Spoon mixture over biscuits. Top with sifted cocoa, then sifted sugar. Let sit at least 1 hour before serving.
Serves 4–6.

Black and Tan Cookies

The kids love these easy and yummy treats.

12 shortbread cookies
½ cup creamy peanut butter
½ cup chocolate–hazelnut spread

Using a spreading knife or spoon, coat half the cookie in peanut butter. With a separate spreading knife or spoon, coat the other half of the cookie in chocolate–hazelnut spread. Repeat with remaining cookies.
Serves 4-6.

Peach–Raspberry "Cobblers"

A fresh, aromatic, no-bake version of the all-American favorite.

15.25 oz (1 can) canned peach halves
    in heavy syrup, drained
4 oz canned red raspberries in heavy syrup, syrup reserved
3 tbsp walnuts
½ cup granola
2 tbsp orange–blossom water
1 tbsp honey
1 tbsp raspberry syrup
⅛ tsp cinnamon

Combine peaches, raspberries, and walnuts in medium–sized bowl. In a screw–top jar, combine orange–blossom water, honey, raspberry syrup and cinnamon and shake vigorously. Pour over fruit mixture and toss. Spoon mixture evenly into dessert bowls. Top with granola.
Serves 4.

Rose Water—scented Pistachio Pudding

With exotic rose water and pistachios, no one will ever believe this is an instant pudding.

> 3.4 oz (1 box) pistachio instant pudding
> 1 ½ cup (1 can) evaporated milk
> ¼ cup water
> 3 tbsp rose water
> 2 tbsp roasted pistachios, shelled
> 3 tbsp dried cranberries
> 4 tbsp graham cracker crumbs

Combine milk, water, and rose water in a medium-sized bowl. Stir instant pudding into milk mixture with wire whisk or hand beater until mixture is well blended and beginning to thicken. Chop the pistachios and cranberries in the food chopper and stir into pudding mix. Line dessert bowls with 1 tbsp each graham cracker crumbs. Pour pudding into bowls. Let set for 1 hour before serving. *Serves 4.*

Raisin–Date Nut Balls

Make as suggested or try a variation using chocolate chips, M&Ms, almonds, etc.

> 5 graham crackers, crushed
> ½ cup raisins
> ½ cup pitted dates, chopped
> ½ cup walnuts, chopped
> ½ cup honey

Mix all ingredients until coated with the honey. Roll into balls. *Serves 4.*

Oranges with Grand Marnier and Cinnamon

Simple but elegant.

1 orange, peeled and sliced into rounds
2 tbsp Grand Marnier
cinnamon

Arrange orange slices on two dessert plates. Sprinkle each slice with Grand Marnier. Top with cinnamon to taste. Let marinate for 20 minutes before serving.
Serves 2.

If you don't have the space or ability to grow citrus or fruit trees outdoors, consider growing them in containers indoors. Though the fruit crops will not be as prolific, they are better than nothing. Besides, many of these trees are highly ornamental. Be sure to place plants where they can get plenty of sunlight (western or southern exposure is recommended), and water only as needed (when the surface of the soil is dry). Do not overfertilize, as this can lead to poor fruit quality and overgrowth of foliage.

Aunt Poppy's Peach–Raspberry Torte

This dessert was inspired by childhood memories. A favorite aunt made a similar version of this torte using fresh peaches during the harvest.

> 24 (approx., depending on size) tea biscuits
> 30 oz (2 cans) canned sliced cling peaches, well drained
> 1 cup table cream
> 6 tbsp raspberry preserves
> ½ cup dried raspberries

Line bottom of 8 x 8 x 2 pan with two layers of tea biscuits. Layer peach slices on top of biscuits. Using a wire whisk, blend cream and preserves together until smooth and creamy. Spread cream mixture over the peaches. Top with dried raspberries. Let set for 1 hour before serving.

Serves 4–6.

Poached Ginger Figs

A Port wine infusion turns standard dried figs into an elegant dessert. On a fair-weather day, these are perfect with cheese.

> 12–14 dried Mission figs
> 1 tbsp Port wine
> 1 tbsp fresh lemon juice
> 2 tbsp water
> 1 tbsp fresh ginger, peeled and minced
> ½ tsp cinnamon
> 1 tbsp honey
> 2 tbsp crystallized ginger, cut into strips

Arrange figs in a small, shallow bowl. Place wine, lemon juice, water, ginger, and honey in screw-top jar and shake vigorously, ensuring honey is fully incorporated. Pour Port mixture over figs. Dust with cinnamon. Let marinate for 1 hour. Before serving, add crystallized ginger strips.

Serves 4.

Storm Gourmet Hurricane Lore
Gold
Rush

*L*egend has it hurricanes cause long-buried Spanish coins to wash up on the beach. The surge apparently dislodges the gold doubloons and silver pieces of eight from the sand.

Beverages

It's wise to stay hydrated in a
stressful situation, so splash into
these refreshing possibilities.
Though this chapter does include
some alcoholic libations, it is best
to limit alcohol intake in a time of
crisis. Always drink responsibly.

The Hurricane

This New Orleans favorite was invented at Pat O'Brien's, a local watering hole. This is the authentic Pat O's recipe, printed with permission.

>   4 oz Pat O'Brien's Rum*
>   4 oz Pat O'Brien's Hurricane Mix*
>   orange wedge
>   maraschino cherry

In a martini shaker, combine rum and Hurricane mix and shake vigorously. Pour into hurricane (hourglass–shaped) glass. Garnish with orange and cherry.

* Rum and mix may be purchased at Pat O'Brien's: (800) 597-4823 or www. patobriens.com. Alternatively, any premium dark rum and passion-fruit juice may be substituted.

Café Frappé

A perennial favorite from the sidewalk cafés of Europe.

>   1 cup water
>   2 tbsp instant coffee (more if you
>   prefer a stronger beverage)
>   1 tbsp sugar
>   ¼ cup evaporated milk

Combine all ingredients in a martini shaker and shake vigorously. Coffee should have a foam head. Pour liquid into a mug, and spoon foam on top.

Spiced Coffee

Spices and orange peel make ordinary coffee an exotic treat.

1 cup water
2 tbsp instant coffee (more if you
     prefer a stronger beverage)
1 tbsp Kahlua coffee liqueur
¼ cup orange peel
½ tsp whole cloves
¼ tsp cinnamon

Stir coffee into water until completely dissolved. Add Kahlua, orange peel, cloves and cinnamon. Let sit for 1 hour for ingredients to meld. Strain into coffee mug.

Mock Sangria

This is the nonalcoholic version of the Spanish wine-and-fruit classic.

4 cups white grape juice
½ cup canned fruit cocktail
½ cup orange sections
1 lemon, sliced
few sprigs of mint

Place grape juice into a pitcher. Add fruit cocktail, orange sections, lemon, and mint. Let infusion sit for 1 hour before serving.
Serves 4.

Cranberry–Lime Fizz

Tart and refreshing!

> 2 cups cranberry juice cocktail
> 2 cups lime–flavored seltzer water
> 1 tbsp fresh lime juice
> lime wedges for garnishing

Combine first three ingredients in a pitcher. Pour into individual glasses and garnish with lime wedges.
Serves 4.

What's in a Name?

A lime is a lime, right? Not if it's a Key lime. Much smaller and thinner skinned than its Persian counterpart, the Key lime was originally introduced by Christopher Columbus to Hispaniola. From there, Spaniards brought it to the Florida Keys, where it thrived until hurricanes destroyed the crops. Key limes still grow in south Florida, but not in groves. Most Key limes now come from Mexico.

Spiced Red Wine

This Scandinavian recipe is courtesy of some Finnish friends who let us in on their little "secrets."

750 ml bottle of Burgundy or Merlot wine
¼ cup Port wine
¼ cup orange peel, coarsely chopped
2 tbsp whole cloves
6 cinnamon sticks

For serving:
4 cinnamon sticks
¼ cup golden raisins
¼ cup slivered almonds

Combine wine, Port, orange peel, cloves, and cinnamon sticks in a bowl or pitcher. Let sit for 1 hour or more to allow ingredients to meld. Strain into small glasses or cups. Add a few raisins and almonds into each cup. Garnish with cinnamon stick.
Serves 4.

Herbed Ginger Soda

Ginger has long been touted for its health benefits—we just like it for its zing factor.

2 cups club soda
2 tbsp fresh lemon juice
1 tbsp ginger, peeled and minced
few sprigs mint

Combine soda, lemon juice, and ginger in a small pitcher and stir. Pour into glasses and garnish with mint.
Serves 2.

Pineapple–Guava Cocktail

A sweet concoction to enjoy during lazy days in the tropics.

> 2 cups pineapple juice
> 2 cups guava nectar
> 1 cup club soda
> pineapple chunks and maraschino cherries for garnishing

Combine pineapple juice and nectar in a pitcher and stir well. Add club soda. Pour into individual glasses and garnish with pineapple and cherry.
Serves 4.

Limeade

Sunny days and cool, refreshing limeade go hand in hand.

> 2 cups sugar
> 1 gallon water
> 2 cups lime juice
> lime wedges for garnishing

Combine water, sugar and lime juice in a pitcher. Stir until sugar is completely dissolved. Pour into tall glasses and garnish with lime wedges.
Serves 6–8.

Spicy Bloody Mary

Equally delicious as a nonalcoholic beverage, or Virgin Mary. Simply omit the vodka.

    1 ½ oz vodka
    3 oz tomato juice
    1 tbsp lemon juice
    ½ tsp Worcestershire sauce
    salt and pepper to taste
    Tabasco to taste
    lime wedges for garnishing

Combine all ingredients except lime wedges in a martini shaker and shake vigorously. Pour into individual glasses and garnish with lime wedge, if desired.

Storm Gourmet Hurricane Lore
Animal
Instinct

Before the advent of sophisticated storm tracking devices and warning systems, islanders and coastal residents watched the behavior of animals for clues of impending storms. Some old-timers watched swans: If they flew toward the wind, a hurricane was sure to strike within twenty-four hours. Bermudans believed that the silk spider predicted stormy weather by spinning its web closer to the ground. In the Carolinas, the locals were convinced a hurricane was coming when shorebirds gathered and livestock wandered.

Appendix I

Refrigerated Foods
To Keep or Not to Keep

*I*f electricity is disrupted for extended periods of time, the safety of refrigerated and frozen foods will become an issue. What is safe to consume? What can be refrozen when the power is restored? What must be thrown away?

The magic number for refrigerated foods is 40°F. Eggs, meats, fish, poultry, and dairy products should be kept at or below this temperature to avoid spoilage and food–borne illness. The chart on this page tells you how to handle foods if the appliance thermometer rises above 40°F for longer than two hours. Most foods that are indicated "Safe" will be fine outside of the refrigerator for days or even weeks. Just use common sense here: If slime, mold, or foul odors develop, discard immediately.

Refrigerated Foods

Fresh Food	*Held above 40°F for over two hours*
Meat, poultry, seafood (including raw and leftover cooked foods)	**Discard**
Thawing meat or poultry	**Discard**
Meat, tuna, shrimp, chicken, or egg salad	**Discard**
Lunchmeats, bacon, hot dogs, sausage	**Discard**

Fresh Food	Held above 40°F for over two hours
Canned hams, meats, and fish, opened	**Discard**
Soft cheeses (ricotta, mozzarella, blue, Brie, Camembert, cottage, cream)	**Discard**
Hard cheeses (Parmesan, Romano, Swiss, cheddar, provolone)	**Safe**
Grated Parmesan/Romano	**Safe**
Shredded cheeses	**Discard**
Baby formula, opened	**Discard**
Milk and cream, all types	**Discard**
Butter, margarine	**Safe**
Eggs, fresh and cooked	**Discard**
Custards, puddings	**Discard**
Fruit juices, opened	**Safe**
Fresh fruits, cut	**Discard**
Canned fruits, opened	**Safe**
Dried or candied fruits	**Safe**
Casseroles, soups, stews	**Discard**
Mayonnaise, tartar sauce, horseradish, opened	**Discard if over 50°F for more than eight hours**
Peanut butter	**Safe**

Fresh Food	*Held above 40°F for over two hours*
Jelly, mustard, ketchup, olives, pickles	**Discard**
Vinegar–based dressings, opened	**Discard**
Creamy dressings, opened	**Discard**
Spaghetti sauce, opened	**Discard**
BBQ, soy, Worcestershire sauce	**Safe**
Fish sauce	**Discard**
Breads, tortillas, cakes, muffins	**Safe**
Refrigerator biscuits, cookie dough	**Discard**
Cooked pasta, rice, potatoes	**Discard**
Pasta salads	**Discard**
Cheesecake	**Discard**
Cream pies or pastries	**Discard**
Fruit pies	**Safe**
Vegetables, raw	**Safe**
Greens, pre–washed, packaged	**Discard**
Vegetables, cooked; tofu	**Discard**
Baked potatoes	**Discard**
Potato salad	**Discard**

Fresh Food	Held above 40°F for over two hours
Vegetable juice, opened	**Discard**
Herbs, spices	**Safe**

Frozen Foods

Fresh Food	Still Contains Ice Crystals	Thawed, held above 40°F for over two hours
Meat, poultry, seafood, pork (including ground)	**Refreeze**	**Discard**
Casseroles, soups, stews	**Refreeze**	**Discard**
Ice cream, frozen yogurt	**Refreeze**	**Discard**
Hard cheeses	**Refreeze**	**Refreeze**
Shredded cheeses	**Refreeze**	**Discard**
Cheesecake	**Refreeze**	**Discard**
Milk	**Refreeze**	**Discard**
Eggs/egg products	**Refreeze**	**Discard**
Fruit juices	**Refreeze**	**Refreeze (discard if mold, smell, or slimi-ness develops)**
Vegetable juices	**Refreeze**	**Discard**
Pie crusts, bread dough	**Refreeze**	**Discard**

Fresh Food	Still Contains Ice Crystals	Thawed, held above 40°F for over two hours
Breakfast items (waffles, pancakes, bagels)	**Refreeze**	**Discard**
Frozen meals	**Refreeze**	**Discard**
Breads, rolls, muffins, cakes (no filling)	**Refreeze**	**Refreeze**
Cakes, pies, pastries (custard or cheese filling)	**Refreeze**	**Discard**
Flour, cornmeal, nuts	**Refreeze**	**Refreeze**

Sources:
1. *"Emergency Preparedness: Keeping Food Safe During an Emergency," United States Department of Agriculture, Food Safety and Inspection Service. www.fsis.usda.gov/factsheets/ keeping_food_safe_during_an_emergency/index.asp Charts printed with permission.*
2. *"Food Safety in Hurricanes and Floods," Home & Garden Information Center, Clemson Extension, Clemson University.*

Storm Gourmet Hurricane Lore
Mind the Gap

*B*et you never thought a hurricane could create a fifty-foot-wide channel of water. In 1819, it did. A great hurricane plowed into the Caribbean island of St. Maarten, washing away all but three houses in the village of Simpson Bay. The storm surge carved a massive channel, effectively isolating the village from the rest of the island. For one hundred and fourteen years the only way to reach Simpson Bay was to take a boat across the lagoon and then follow a path through a mangrove swamp. A bridge was finally built in 1933 to reconnect the village to St. Maarten.

Appendix II
Substitutions

While many recipes call for fresh fruit, citrus juices, and herbs, some of these items may not be readily available during the course of a storm. The chart below lists substitutions for most of the fresh or perishable items used in *The Storm Gourmet* recipes. Keep in mind the substitutes will not be as intensely flavored and may alter the taste of the final product.

Fresh Food	Substitute	Amount Sub. = Fresh
Lemon juice	**Bottled juice**	**Same**
Lime juice	**Bottled juice**	**Same**
Key lime juice	**Bottled juice**	**Same**
Lemon zest	*None*	
Lime zest	*None*	
Orange zest	*None*	
Orange juice	**Commercially packaged juice**	**Same**
Orange	**Jarred orange sections**	**1 cup = 1 orange**
	Mandarin orange sections	**1 cup = 1 orange**

Fresh Food	Substitute	Amount Sub. = Fresh
Grapefruit	**Canned/jarred grapefruit**	**2 cups = 1 grape-fruit**
Mango	**Dried mango**	**½ dried=1 fresh**
	Canned mango	**Same**
Avocado	***None***	
Mint	**Dried mint flakes**	**½ dried=1 fresh**
Chives	**Dried chives**	**½ dried=1 fresh**
Cilantro	**Dried cilantro flakes**	**½ dried=1 fresh**
Basil	**Dried basil**	**½ dried=1 fresh**
Parsley (curly or Italian)	**Dried parsley flakes**	**½ dried=1 fresh**
Dill	**Dried dill**	**½ dried=1 fresh**
Garlic	**Commercially packaged garlic**	**Same**
Ginger	**Dried ginger**	**½ dried=1 fresh**
Onion	**Dehydrated onion**	**½ dried=1 fresh**

Note: *Substitutions are not recommended for: Lemon Herb Pasta, Pesto Pasta, Pesto and Chickpea Spread, Valerie's Tuna Cannellini.*

Storm Gourmet Hurricane Lore
Untying the Knot

If you think your mother is superstitious, you have never met a sailor. Seafarers have a long list of super-stitions, especially when it comes to the sea. According to sailing legend, the tying and untying of certain knots controlled the power of the wind. They would begin by tying three knots. Untying the first would produce a moderate wind; the second would lead to a stronger gale; and the third would unleash the fury of a hurricane.

Index

If you enjoyed this book, here are some other Pineapple Press titles you might enjoy as well. To request our complete catalog or to place an order, write to Pineapple Press, P.O. Box 3889, Sarasota, Florida 34230, or call 1–800–PINEAPL (746–3275). Or visit our website at www.pineapplepress.com.

The Essential Catfish Cookbook by Janet Cope and Shannon Harper. Mouth-watering recipes that call for succulent catfish and a variety of easy-to-find ingredients. Learn about the private life of the captivating catfish and enjoy this Southern delicacy. (pb)

Exotic Foods: A Kitchen & Garden Guide by Marian Van Atta. Grow avocado, mango, carambola, guava, kiwi, pomegranate, and other rare delights in your subtropical backyard. Includes planting and growing instructions as well as over one hundred recipes for enjoying your bountiful crops. (pb)

Mastering the Art of Florida Seafood by Lonnie T. Lynch. Includes tips on purchasing, preparing, and serving fish and shellfish—with alligators thrown in for good measure. Also includes instructions for artistic food placement, food painting techniques, and more. (pb)

The Mongo Mango Cookbook by Cynthia Thuma. Much more than a book of easy-to-make recipes, this book is also a compendium of mango history, legend, and literature. It traces the fragrant fruit's genesis and its proliferation throughout the world's warm climates, and explains why the mango's versatility and palate-pleasing flavor make it a favorite among chefs. (pb)

The Mostly Mullet Cookbook by George "Grif" Griffin. Mulletheads unite! Includes dozens of mullet main dishes, such as Dixie Fried Mullet, Mullet Italiano, Sweet & Sour Mullet, and the Sea Dog Sandwich, as well as mullet-friendly sides and sauces and other great Southern seafood, including Judy's Mullet Butter and Ybor City Street Vendor's Crab Cakes. (pb)

The Sunshine State Cookbook by George S. Fichter. Delicious ways to enjoy the familiar and exotic fruits and vegetables that abound in Florida all year round. Includes seafood cooking tips and delectable recipes such as Rummed Pineapple Flambé and Caribbean Curried Lobster. (pb)

Tropical Surge by Benjamin Reilly. This engaging historical narrative covers many significant events in the history of south Florida. Reilly tells the story of the battle between human ambition and hurricanes, and includes gripping narratives of the 1919, 1926, and 1935 hurricanes in south Florida and the Keys. (hb)